A *TIGER* AND A *FUSILIER*

LEICESTER'S VC HEROES

**Private William H Buckingham VC,
2nd Battalion, The Leicestershire Regiment.**
(Record Office for Leicestershire, Leicester & Rutland)

**Captain Robert Gee, VC, MC,
2nd Battalion, The Royal Fusiliers.**
(The Royal Fusiliers Museum)

"Then was seen with what a strength and majesty the British soldier fights"
Sir William Napier (1785-1860)
British General and Historian

DEREK SEATON

First published 2001 by Derek Seaton
Botcheston, Leics

Copyright © Derek Seaton 2001

ISBN 0-9528948-2-3

Printed in Great Britain by Norwood Press, Anstey, Leicester
Design and Layout by Robin Stevenson, Kairos Press, Newtown Linford, Leicester
Body text in Century Schoolbook BT, 11pt.

British Library Cataloguing in Publication Data
A catalogue record for this book is available from the British Library

Photographs on rear cover:

Monument to the 29th Division, Stretton-on-Dunsmore, Warwickshire.
(DEREK SEATON)

Memorial to the Royal Leicestershire Regiment, The War Memorial, Victoria Park, Leicester.
(DEREK SEATON)

By the same author:

Light amid the Shadows:	The History of the Royal Leicestershire, Rutland and Wycliffe Society for the Blind 1858-1993
The Local Legacy of Thomas Cook	
From Strength to Strength:	The History of the first 100 years of the Leicester, Leicestershire and Rutland Guild for Disabled People 1898-1998
From Tollgate To Tramshed:	The History of London Road, Leicester c1860-1920 (Helen Boynton and Derek Seaton)

FOREWORD

A TIGER AND A FUSILIER

It is a pleasure to write a Foreword to this fascinating and rather humbling story of two Leicestershire soldiers whose lives, whilst linked by schooling and military distinction, followed quite different paths.

Derek Seaton is to be congratulated on his patient and diligent research, and the careful checking of information from a variety of sources, which has ensured such an accurate final record. The result is an intriguing story of both disadvantage and kindness, and of hardship and bravery, which begins in the reign of Queen Victoria and ends in the days of the Commonwealth.

It reminds us of two local heroes whose exploits made such an impact on the people of Leicester and Leicestershire of their day and who are now deservedly brought to our notice in this most interesting book.

Major Geoffrey G Simpson TD DL
Chairman
Leicestershire and Rutland Committee
East Midlands Reserve Forces and Cadets
Association

31 July 2001

PREFACE

For a number of years I have been fascinated by the exploits of Private William Buckingham, VC and Captain Robert Gee, VC, MC. Both were casualties of the harsh Victorian era which resulted in them being received into the care of the Board of Guardians as young boys. After being placed in local workhouses each of them was admitted to the Countesthorpe Cottage Homes in Leicestershire. From there they, together with a number of other boys, from the Cottage Homes, joined the Army as regular soldiers.

Their paths did not cross but their deeds, on the battlefields of the Western Front, ran in parallel and resulted in each of them standing before their Sovereign to receive the world's most coveted award for gallantry. One was a natural leader of men who inspired young soldiers, half his age, by his acts of bravery. The other was fearless in his determination to save his wounded comrades from certain death. Both showed a total disregard for their own safety, and their achievements, which were truly inspirational, characterised all that is best in the redoubtable British soldier.

Their stories are remarkable and deserve to be recorded for posterity before they are lost in the mists of time. It is to the memory of these two gallant soldiers that I proudly dedicate '*A Tiger And A Fusilier*'.

Derek Seaton

CONTENTS

Foreword iii

Preface iv

Acknowledgements vii

THE TIGER 1

1. The Makings of a Tiger 2

2. For King and Country 13

THE FUSILIER 29

3. A Soldier of the Queen 30

4. Comrades in Arms 35

5. Soldier to Politician 50

6. A New Lease of Life 61

Appendices 74

Bibliography 77

Index 78

ACKNOWLEDGEMENTS

My sincere thanks are extended to a great many people and organisations who have so generously contributed of their knowledge and time, without which I could not have written *A Tiger and A Fusilier*.

I am very grateful indeed to the following:

The Bedfordshire and Luton Archives and Records Service for access to important material relating to the early life of William Buckingham and his family.

The Imperial War Museum where I was able to peruse the extensive files on both Private Buckingham and Captain Gee, also for kind permission to use relevant photographs.

Staff of the National Army Museum, Chelsea, for making available the Lummis files – a wonderful collection of data, on the VC holders, compiled with enormous care and dedication by the Reverend Canon William Murrell Lummis, MC who served as a Captain in the Suffolk Regiment.

Carl Harrison, Chief Archivist, The Record Office for Leicestershire, Leicester & Rutland for permission to use a range of photographs. Particular thanks are due to Adam Goodwin who provided me with a great deal of assistance and to Robin Jenkins for locating a number of wonderful, hitherto unpublished photographs.

James P. Kelleher, Archivist, The Royal Fusiliers Museum and Archives, City of London Headquarters, The Royal Regiment of Fusiliers, HM Tower of London for access to the files relating to Captain Gee, the War Diaries of the 2nd Battalion, Royal Fusiliers and for permission to use a number of important photographs. My thanks also go to Jim for the warmth of his welcome whenever I visited the traditional home of the Royal Fusiliers housed in such a magnificent location.

Colonel F.A.H. Swallow OBE, Secretary of the Royal Tigers' Association, the Royal Leicestershire Regiment for valuable information, from the regimental history archive, regarding Private William Buckingham.

Officers of the Leicester City Council – Angela Cutting and Joyce Mills, Community History, Leicester City Libraries, for locating and making available a number of photographs, Charles Poole, Assistant Town Clerk (Corporate Services), and colleagues, for permission to use photographs of a number of former Lord Mayors and to quote from minutes and reports of the City Council. Also to Kim Bromley-Derry, Assistant Director of Social Services for the updated history of the Buckingham VC Memorial Fund.

Nick Carter the Editor of the *Leicester Mercury* for his assistance and encouragement and for permission to use a number of photographs which appeared in the *Leicester Mercury*, the *Leicester Evening Mail* and *Leicester Daily Post*. To Steve England and the staff of the *Leicester Mercury* Library and to Mr Leicester for early references to my work.

Diane Chalmers, Editor and Mitch Irving of *The Hinckley Times* for enabling me to access research material relating to Captain Robert Gee and for the use of a number of photographs.

Paul Oldfield, military historian and writer, who is currently compiling a two-volume biographical account of the British land forces VC winners of the Western Front in the First World War and to Jim Underwood, former Colonel, Royal Australian Army and military historian. Both provided a considerable amount of detailed information which proved to be immensely valuable.

The Heritage House Group Ltd, Derby, News International Syndication (on behalf of *The Times*) and *The West Australian* (West Australian Newspapers Ltd) for permission to use important photographs.

The staff of the Australian High Commission, London for detailed information regarding Perth and the area of Western Australia upon which part of my research was focused.

Three local historians have given me a great deal of their time, provided a wealth of information and allowed me to use many of their photographs; for all of this my sincere thanks go to Dr Clive Harrison, Henrietta Schultka and John Taylor.

I am also indebted to the following for their important contributions and, in a number of instances, for allowing me to take copies of their photographs:

Josie Adcock, C.E. John Aston, Shirley Aucott, June Bailey, Ben Beazley, J.D. Bennett, Anthony Cain, Sue Dobby, Greg Drodz, Peter Foster, Doug Gee, Peter Holmes, Brian Kibble, Peter Lowe, Duncan Lucas, Michael Roberts, Karen Saunders, Margaret Shaw, Dr Joan Skinner, Stuart T. Swann, Michael Tedd, Arthur Tomlin, Stan Vaughan, the Reverend Kenneth Wayne and Pat Wilson.

Every effort has been made to trace the copyright holder of the picture of Captain Gee which appeared in The War Illustrated, but without success. I apologise in advance for any unintentional omission. I would be pleased to insert the appropriate acknowledgement in any subsequent edition of this publication.

A very special word of thanks has to go to Captain Robert Gee's grandchildren, Robert N. Harrison and Margaret Self for the very considerable assistance they have so willingly given to me. Robert Harrison has provided me with a wealth of information and anecdotes about his grandfather which, together with a range of photographs he has made available, has played a vital part in piecing together the life of Captain Gee. He also kindly read the draft chapters of both The Tiger and The Fusilier and offered me a great deal of sound advice in terms of amending and improving the contents.

My grateful thanks go to Major Geoffrey G. Simpson, TD, DL, of the Royal Tigers' Association for his great kindness in writing the Foreword to this volume.

It remains for me to say a very big thank you to Josie Bicker for proofreading the entire manuscript with enthusiasm and eagle-eyed proficiency, her contribution was invaluable.

Finally, if I have, inadvertently, omitted anyone from the acknowledgements who contributed to the gathering of material for *A Tiger and A Fusilier* please accept my apology. You can be assured of my gratitude.

Permission to use photographs on the front cover is gratefully acknowledged as follows:
The Victoria Cross The Royal Regiment of Fusiliers transparency is by kind permission of Heritage House Group Ltd.
Private William Buckingham, VC Photograph by kind permission of the Record Office for Leicestershire, Leicester & Rutland.
Captain Robert Gee, VC, MC Photograph courtesy of the Imperial War Museum, London. (Q80673)

THE TIGER

Private William Henry Buckingham, VC 2nd Battalion, The Leicestershire Regiment.
(PHOTOGRAPH COURTESY OF THE IMPERIAL WAR MUSEUM, LONDON. Q79790)

The 17th (Leicestershire) Regiment of Foot was ordered to India in 1804 where it remained for nineteen years. On 25 June 1825, His Majesty King George IV approved the Regiment to bear "on its colours and appointments the figure of the 'ROYAL TIGER' with the word 'HINDOOSTAN' superscribed, as a lasting testimony of the exemplary conduct of the Corps during the period of service in India from 1804 to 1823."

1
THE MAKINGS OF A TIGER

William Henry Buckingham – later to become affectionately known as Billy Buckingham – was born at 57 St John's Street, Bedford on 29 March 1886. His real name was William Henry Billington and he was the first child of William John Billington, a market gardener and Annie Susan Billington (née Bennett). The cottage where the family lived stood in the shadow of the Parish Church of St John.

Both parents were natives of Bedfordshire, William John Billington was born at Flitwick in 1869 and his wife Annie was born in Bedford in the spring of 1867. The young couple were married at the Parish Church of St Cuthbert, Mill Street, Bedford on 1 February 1886.

The church of St Cuthbert was named after Saint Cuthbert (635-687) Bishop of Lindisfarne and is situated on the east side of the town. (The church now serves as the Polish Roman Catholic Church of the Sacred Heart of Jesus and St Cuthbert).

A second son was born to William and Annie Billington at 14 Bower Street, Bedford, on 7 May 1887, and named Frederick Ernest Billington. Tragedy was soon to follow for the young Billington family when, on 5 March 1888, the father and breadwinner died at New Spring Road, Kempston, a village nearby, at the early age of 19 years. The cause of death was phthisis (pulmonary tuberculosis). The bringing up of two small sons was, clearly, a burden for Annie Billington. By May 1889 the family was living at Howbury Street, Bedford and was receiving outdoor relief from the local Board of Guardians. Consideration was given to taking Frederick into the Bedford Union Workhouse but, in the event, it was William Billington, then aged 3 years, who was admitted to the Workhouse on 17 May 1889. The reason for his admission

Right: The Parish Church of St John, St John's Street, Bedford.
(DEREK SEATON)

Below: St Cuthbert's Church, Mill Street, Bedford.
(DEREK SEATON)

Bedford Union Workhouse, Kimbolton Street, Bedford.
(DEREK SEATON)

was that his mother was no longer able to adequately care for him.

The Bedford Union Workhouse, situated in Kimbolton Road, was erected in 1796 as the House of Industry. The building was subsequently let to the Guardians of the Poor in 1835.

The Workhouse was a large brick building with a chapel and schoolrooms. It was capable of accommodating 400 inmates, although by 1890 there were less than 200 people there. The Master was George Croxton Walker and his wife was the Matron. Other members of the staff included a Schoolmaster, a Schoolmistress and an Assistant Schoolmistress.

The Workhouse Infirmary became St Peter's Hospital on 5 July 1948 and later formed the North Wing of Bedford General Hospital.

When the 1891 National Census was taken, William remained in the Workhouse whereas his brother Frederick was living with his maternal grandparents Joab and Flora Bennett at 14 Bower Street, Bedford. At the age of 4 years, William was one of the youngest inmates in Bedford Workhouse at that time.

Meanwhile, William's mother had left Bedford to go to Leicester in order to obtain work as a shoe fitter and was living in lodgings at 16 Park Street, Leicester the home of Mrs Elizabeth Trippe, a widow, and her daughter Emma. Whilst in Leicester, Annie Billington met Thomas Henry Buckingham, the 18 years old son of Jacob and Ann Buckingham of 21 Upper Charles Street in the town. He was a shoe riveter and it is likely that they met whilst working in a local factory. They were married at Holy Trinity Parish

Holy Trinity Church, Regent Road, Leicester.
(DEREK SEATON)

Court A an adjoining court in Upper Charles Street, Leicester 1929.
(LEICESTER MERCURY)

Church, Regent Road, Leicester on 3 August 1891.

The Buckinghams lived in a tiny two-roomed cottage at 9 Court C, Upper Charles Street near to the parents of Thomas Buckingham.

A son was born to the newly married Buckinghams on 19 November 1891 at their small dwelling, off Upper Charles Street, and he was named Joseph Henry Buckingham. Problems were again encountered by Annie Buckingham, in caring for her infant son, and the baby was admitted to the Leicester Union Workhouse, Sparkenoe Street, Leicester on 21 April 1892. He remained there until he was taken out by his parents, some three weeks later, on 14 May 1892.

At the same time news had reached the Board of Guardians at Bedford of Annie Billington's marriage to Thomas Buckingham and enquiries were ordered to be made regarding "the circumstances of the stepfather of William Billington, an inmate in the (Bedford) Workhouse and the child's settlement." On 28 May 1892 the Workhouse Master at Bedford, was instructed to hand over both William and his brother Frederick to their mother and stepfather living in Leicester. He was also ordered to communicate with the Leicester Union Workhouse on the matter. Shortly afterwards, on 11 June 1892, the Clerk to the Bedford Board of Guardians was directed "to take the necessary steps to remove William Billington to Leicester, the place of his settlement, where his mother and stepfather now reside." Matters rapidly deteriorated and Annie Buckingham and her seven month old son were admitted to Leicester Union Workhouse on 20 June 1892. The reason for her admission was given as "neglected by her husband." One week later William and Frederick were brought from Bedford to join their mother and half-brother Joseph in Leicester Workhouse.

The entry in the Admission and Discharge Book of the Leicester Union Workhouse shows the details of the admission of the two young brothers:

27 June 1892
    Buckingham William Henry
        C/E   born 1886
    Buckingham Frederick Ernest
        C/E   born 1887
    Transferred from Bedford.
    Mother in House.

Thus, it transpired that from the date of his admission to the Leicester Union Workhouse, William Billington became William Buckingham taking the surname of his Leicester-born stepfather, someone whom he had never known and, furthermore someone who had not been involved in his care and upbringing. His brother Frederick also took the surname of Buckingham.

The Leicester Union Workhouse was designed by the local architect William Flint and was built in 1839, by the Leicester Board of Guardians, to accommodate 650 people. The building was enlarged in 1851 to provide accommodation for 1000 paupers. Visually a striking building, its main entrance was described in the following terms: "The front elevation is peculiarly judicious, having a neat homely English appearance and nothing of the character of a Bastille." (*Leicester Chronicle* 4 November 1839).

The Public Assistance Committee of the Leicester City Council replaced the Board of Guardians in 1930 and the former Workhouse became Hillcrest Welfare Establishment & Hospital on 5 July 1948. The building was eventually demolished in 1977.

A further move for William and Frederick Buckingham came on 15 July 1892 when they were discharged from the Leicester Union Workhouse to the Countesthorpe Cottage Homes, a comparatively new and progressive development situated some three-quarters of a mile west of the village of Countesthorpe, six miles due south of Leicester

The Cottage Homes were built in 1884 by the Leicester Board of Guardians for pauper children of the Leicester Union "to be used for the reception of poor children belonging to the Union." They were designed by the Leicester architect Isaac Barradale (1845-1892) and were formally opened on 26 November 1884 by Edward Barrand Pipes, a local builder and chairman of the Leicester Board of Guardians. The site of the Countesthorpe Cottage Homes and grounds covered 55 acres, the cost of which was £6,200, and the buildings consisted of the following:

8 cottages for 24 children	192
2 cottages for 16 children	32
1 Infants cottage	30
Total:	254

In addition there were schools, workshops, stores, an infirmary (20 beds) an isolation unit (10 beds), a swimming bath, a boiler house, laundry and water-tower plus an additional cottage which served as the residence for the Superintendent and Matron. They had responsibility for the management of the Cottage Homes and were directly accountable to the Leicester Board of Guardians. The cost of the buildings amounted to £23,140 making a total cost of £29,340 for the project in its entirety.

Leicester Union Workhouse Sparkenhoe Street (later Swain Street) Leicester. 1956.
(LEICESTER MERCURY)

The building of the Cottage Homes was both creditable and, in a sense, revolutionary on the part of the local Guardians. Isaac Barradale's attractive design work resulted in a splendid complex of Vernacular or Domestic Revival style dwellings, which contained slightly contrasting architectural features, set in spacious grounds which enabled the architect to position a number of them at different angles.

It was into this entirely new world that William and Frederick Buckingham entered on 15 July 1892 when they were admitted to Cottage No 6. The entry in the Admission Ledger read:

"Mother in Union Infirmary.
Deserted by Father."

Each cottage was in the charge of a resident House Mother who, if married, would be assisted by her husband acting as House Father, added to which he would be employed on the estate. Children attended the school on site until they reached 11 years of age at which point

Cottage No 6.
(DEREK SEATON)

they moved on to the village school in Countesthorpe. Later some of the children were found placements in nearby villages and in various secondary schools in Leicester. There was a farm and several workshops, which served the Cottage Homes, where boys from the age of 11 years upwards could be introduced to trades such as carpentry, painting and decorating, shoemaking and the skills of the tailor. The girls received training in domestic and household affairs which resulted in some of them remaining as House Mothers themselves or going on to enter domestic service upon leaving the care of the Leicester Board of Guardians. The philosophy of the Cottage Homes centred upon the provision of parental care, a sound education plus industrial or domestic training designed to prepare the children to be able to earn a living when the time came for them to be discharged.

Whilst William and Frederick Buckingham were able to experience a degree of relative calm in their young and troubled lives, following their admission to the Cottage Homes, their family problems deepened. Their half-brother Joseph died in Leicester Workhouse on 4 September 1892, aged 9 months, and was buried four days later in a common grave at Welford Road Cemetery, Leicester. Seven weeks later, on 26 October 1892, their mother Annie took her discharge from the Workhouse and her whereabouts then became unknown.

The fairly strict regime at the Cottage Homes, which for some children was quite authoritarian, provided much needed stability and security for the young Buckingham brothers. They would rise with the other children at 6.30 am, at the sound of the bell or bugle, breakfast at 7.30 am and then spend the day at their lessons at the Infant School.

Time would be set aside for recreation, bathing and work in the Trades and Needlework Division before supper at 5.40 pm, which was followed by a final period of recreation prior to the bell or bugle sounding to denote bedtime at 7.30 pm or dusk.

The School, Countesthorpe Cottage Homes.
(DEREK SEATON)

The children were required to attend morning service at the village church on Sunday mornings. They were marched to the Church of St Andrew where they always occupied the same pews, at the side of the church, and were kept separate from the other children of the village. In the afternoon they attended Sunday School in their own schoolroom at the Cottage Homes.

One important stabilising factor in the lives of the Buckingham brothers resulted from the appointment of William and Sarah Jane Harrison as Superintendent and Matron, of the Cottage Homes, in 1896. Both were teachers and were seeking a joint-appointment. Initially they were appointed to their posts for a trial period of twelve months. Not only did they successfully complete this probationary stage but they went on to serve as Superintendent and Matron for 26 years until William Harrison's death, whilst still in post, in June 1922. William Harrison was responsible for the administration and management of the Cottage Homes whilst his wife looked after the general welfare of the children and the supervision of the staff in the cottages. Although Sarah Harrison was a kind person, and extremely efficient, she was held in awe and was, generally, less approachable than her husband. William Harrison was viewed as being a real "father-figure" and was greatly loved by the children who would rush up to him whenever he was seen in the grounds.

William Buckingham's formative years, spent at the Cottage Homes, not only gave him the security of his first real home; they also enabled him to experience the several trade opportunities on offer there. One occupation which interested him was tailoring and he began to learn the rudiments of the trade through the needlework sessions he attended,

He finally took his discharge from the Cottage Homes on 29 November 1901, having decided to make the Army his career. It was on that day that he enlisted in the Leicestershire Regiment (17th Regiment of Foot) at the Regimental Depot, based at the nearby Glen Parva Barracks. No

Above: The Parish Church of St Andrew, Countesthorpe. (DEREK SEATON)
Below: The former residence of the Superintendent and Matron. (DR CLIVE HARRISON)

Entrance to Glen Parva Barracks (built in 1881).
(DUNCAN LUCAS)

6276 Private William Buckingham, aged 15 years and 8 months, at the date of his attestation, joined as a Boy Soldier. His trade was shown as Tailor's Boy and, initially, he signed for a term of 12 years. He was recorded as being 5 feet $2^{1}/_{8}$ inches in height and his weight was given as 98 lbs (7 stone).

The structured environment at the Cottage Homes proved to be a good grounding for boys attracted to life in the Army and the Royal Navy and was invaluable in enabling them to make a relatively smooth transition into the disciplined life of the services. William's younger brother, Frederick was discharged from the Cottage Homes on 11 September 1902 and went on to join the Royal Navy.

Private Buckingham's early years in the Leicestershire Regiment gave him the opportunity "to see the world." On 12 May 1902 he was transferred to the 2nd Battalion, then serving in Egypt, where the battalion had been stationed since its arrival at Alexandria on 18 February 1900. The battalion subsequently embarked at Alexandria, on 30 November 1902, bound for Southampton where it was transferred to Guernsey and Alderney the following day. After almost two years in the Channel Islands the 2nd Battalion was then posted to Colchester, arriving there on 29 September 1904. During the battalion's stay at Colchester Military Garrison, Private Buckingham appeared before his Commanding Officer, on 2 October 1905, and was "awarded" (C.O.'s punishment) 10 days hard labour for misconduct.

Further overseas service was soon to follow when Private Buckingham was transferred to the 1st Battalion of the Leicestershire Regiment, then serving at Belgaum in India, on 28 February 1906. His new unit had been stationed in India since arriving there on 30 November 1902 from South Africa. He was soon to rejoin the 2nd Battalion which sailed from Southampton on 21 September 1906 for Bombay, where it disembarked and proceeded to Belgaum to relieve the 1st Battalion on 13 October. The two battalions were together for three days whereupon Private Buckingham was posted back to the 2nd Battalion on 16 October 1906, the day the 1st Battalion left for Bombay on route to England.

On 28 February 1908, the 2nd Battalion was adjudged "the best Regiment at arms" (British Regiments) in the 6th Divisional "Assault at Arms" held over a five day period at Poona.

The establishment of the 2nd Battalion on 31 December 1910 was as follows:

28	Officers
2	Warrant Officers
45	Sergeants
16	Drummers
40	Corporals
900	Privates
1031	Total strength

In March 1911 the 2nd Battalion was under orders to leave Belgaum for Madras and Bellary. Whilst at Madras Private Buckingham extended his engagement to complete 21 years service with the Colours. He underwent his medical examination on 11 December 1912, was pronounced fit and duly re-engaged. His qualification, at the time, was noted as "Range Finder". After almost two years in Madras the 2nd Battalion sailed for Calcutta on 4 February 1913, on board RMS *Northbrook*. From Calcutta all personnel were transported by rail to Bareilly to join the Bareilly Brigade of the 7th Meerut Division.

Immediately after the declaration of war by Britain against Germany, on 4 August 1914, following the entry of German forces into Belgium, the 2nd Battalion of the Leicestershire Regiment began to prepare for embarkation and subsequent action on the Western Front. On 21 September 1914 the battalion sailed from Karachi on board the *Elephanta* bound for France via Port Said. The battalion disembarked at Marseille on 12 October and moved to La Ventive Camp. The 2nd Battalion formed part of the Garhwal Brigade, of the Meerut Division of the Indian Army Corps, commanded by Lieutenant-General Charles Alexander Anderson. The other Brigades, within the Meerut Division, were the Dehra and Bareilly Brigades. The Garhwal Brigade moved to Calonne on 28 October 1914 where the 2nd Battalion of the Leicestershire Regiment, commanded by Lieutenant-Colonel Charles Guinand Blackader, was to experience its baptism of fire, on the Western Front, at the First Battle of Ypres. The Leicesters occupied the front line trenches, the following day, when they relieved the 3rd Battalion, the Worcestershire Regiment.

Within weeks of the Battalion's arrival on the Western Front, Private William Buckingham had distinguished himself in action and his name had become known to the Corps Commander. On 18 December, at Givenchy, Lieutenant-General Sir James Willcocks, the Commander of the Indian Army Corps reported that: "The following were brought to special notice during these operations: Lieutenant-Colonel Blackader who led his Battalion and withdrew it skilfully, Major Knatchbull, Captain Romily and Lieutenant Tooley, all of the Leicesters: No 6276 Private Buckingham for great gallantry, Sergeant Sutherland, Lance Corporal Brake and Private Crisp; and if all the names of other brave Leicestershire officers and men were recorded here and wherever the Battalion was engaged, they would fill many pages." [*History of the 1st and 2nd Battalions, The Leicestershire Regiment in the Great War* by Colonel Harold Carmichael Wylly CB]. By 22 December the 2nd Battalion had lost 2 officers and 14 other ranks killed plus 2 officers and 73 other ranks wounded. For their operations in the trenches, during December they received due praise from Field-Marshal Sir John French, Commander-in-Chief of the British Expeditionary Force (BEF), who inspected the 2nd Battalion on 7 December, and told the assembled ranks: "I wish personally to thank you for your good work and I am very grateful to you."

During February 1915, Private Buckingham was back in Leicestershire for a short spell of leave. He visited the Cottage Homes and upon leaving he made a significant remark to William Harrison, the Superintendent, when he said: "Well goodbye sir. I'll win the VC or get killed." He then returned to France to rejoin his battalion as it prepared for the British Army's Spring offensive on the Western Front.

The following month the 2nd Battalion, the Leicestershire Regiment was moved into forward positions as General Sir Douglas Haig's 1st Army prepared for the attack on Aubers Ridge. Two Corps were deployed with IV Corps to the north and the Indian Army Corps positioned to the south of Neuve Chapelle respectively. The Indian Army Corps provided the Garhwal Brigade of the Meerut Division for the assault on Neuve Chapelle. The Brigade consisted of five Battalions:

2nd Battalion, Leicestershire Regiment
3rd Battalion, The London Rifles
                (Territorial Force)
1st Battalion, 39th Garhwal Rifles
2nd Battalion, 39th Garhwal Rifles
2nd Battalion, 3rd Gurkha Rifles

The Battle of Neuve Chapelle was about to commence [See Appendix I – The Western Front]

The advance on the village of Neuve Chapelle commenced at 8.05 am on the morning of 10 March with the Garhwal Brigade being positioned south of the village. The 2nd Battalion of the Leicestershire Regiment was allocated a 300 yard sector northward from the junction of Port Arthur on the La Bassée to Estaires Road. The objective was to capture a group of houses, held by the enemy, on the approaches to Neuve Chapelle. In the account of the action, in the battalion's War Diary, it was recorded that the Leicesters quickly overwhelmed the German positions and reached their objective by 8.30 am. The village of Neuve Chapelle was captured, by midday, by the rapidly advancing British and Indian infantry.

By dusk the whole labyrinth of trenches, which extended on a front of some 4000 yards, had been taken by the IV Corps and the Indian Army Corps and a large number of prisoners had been taken during the action. Little progress was made on 11 March when the 2nd Battalion was subjected to German shell fire. The attack was continued but the battalion was, in the main, pinned down in the captured enemy trenches.

At 5.00 pm on 12 March the enemy launched a counter-attack. The Leicesters held their ground and the attack was fiercely resisted with the Germans suffering heavy casualties including several hundred troops killed. The following day saw the 2nd Battalion continuing to hold their trenches but further progress was not possible and General Sir Douglas Haig finally closed down the campaign at 11.00 pm on 12 March. The 2nd Battalion of the Leicestershire Regiment was relieved at midnight on 13 March, its place in the front line being taken by the 1st Battalion, 4th Gurkha Rifles. The Leicesters marched to L'Epinette, through the night, and reached their designated billets at 6.00 am on the morning of 14 March.

The very severe casualties, on both sides, in the short, terrifying Battle of Neuve Chapelle bore witness to the intensity of the action:

British First Army

	Officers	Other Ranks
Killed	190	2,337
Wounded	359	8,174
Missing	23	1,728
	572	12,239

Total casualties: 12,811

The losses incurred by the 6th German Army were estimated at several thousand dead and upwards of 12,000 wounded – an approximate total of 17,000.

Enemy prisoners taken: 30 officers and 1,167 other ranks captured.
                [*Leicester Daily Post*
                15 April 1915]

The casualties suffered by the 2nd Battalion, the Leicestershire Regiment amounted to 250 officers and men of all ranks killed or wounded.

Following the battle, details of acts of gallantry began to emerge. Many examples of selfless heroism, by men of the 2nd Leicesters, were witnessed for which awards were recommended, the greatest honour being accorded to 6276 Private William Buckingham of A Company who was awarded the Victoria Cross. Throughout the three day ordeal he repeatedly went out of the trenches, under very heavy fire, to attend to wounded comrades, a number of whom he rescued and brought to safety. The accounts of his actions, at the time, did not give the names of the men he rescued but it emerged later that they included 16152 Corporal W. Tarry, also of A Company and Private Michael Lane, a Company Signaller also of the 2nd Battalion, both of whom would, otherwise, have perished.

In the heat of the battle Private Buckingham responded to the cries of a

An artist's impression of Private William Buckingham assisting a wounded comrade from the battlefield at Neuve Chapelle.
(PHOTOGRAPH COURTESY OF THE IMPERIAL WAR MUSEUM, LONDON Q79790)

severely wounded German soldier. His description of this event read as follows: "During the battle I came across a badly wounded German soldier, one of his legs had been blown off. He was lying right in the fire-zone and I heard his piteous appeal for help – well I rendered first aid as well as I could and just carried him to a place of safety. Of course I did what I could for others too but it's not worth talking about."

Private Buckingham did not escape unscathed. On 12 March he jumped over a parapet, whilst taking a despatch to his Commanding Officer, when he was shot in the chest. The bullet struck the left side of his chest and was deflected by his paybook, which contained 49 field postcards, in the pocket of his tunic. This caused the bullet to emerge through the right side of his chest where it hit his cartridge case and became embedded in

Private William Buckingham, VC sharing the citation in the morning newspaper with a member of staff and young boy at the Countesthorpe Cottage Homes. (RECORD OFFICE FOR LEICESTERSHIRE, LEICESTER & RUTLAND)

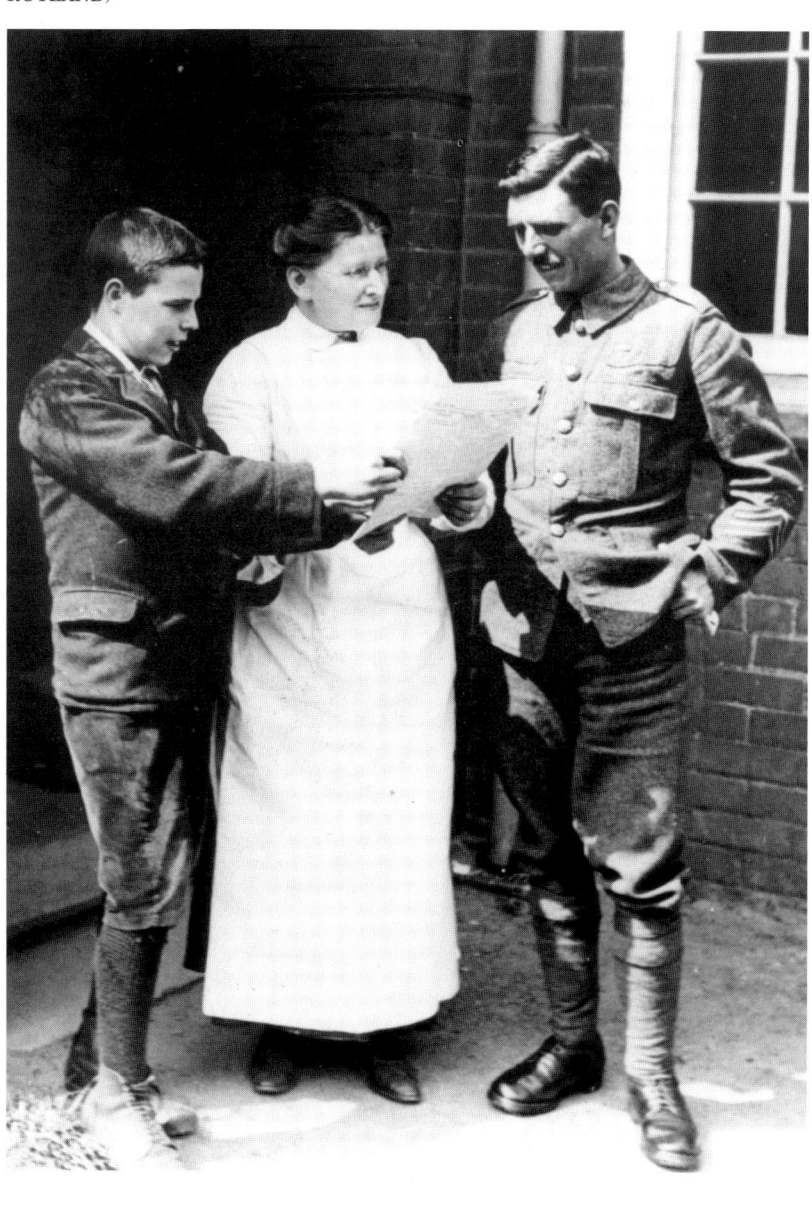

the muscle of his right upper arm. He was evacuated and brought back, with ever growing numbers of wounded comrades, to England. The bullet was removed by surgeons at South Manchester Hospital where, typically, Private Buckingham declined to have chloroform whilst the bullet was extracted.

Following medical treatment he reported back to his Regimental Depot at Glen Parva Barracks and then proceeded to the Countesthorpe Cottage Homes, on 7 April, as the guest of Mr and Mrs William Harrison for a period of convalescence. During all of this time Private Buckingham had no idea that he had been recommended for the Victoria Cross. News of the award was given, through the Press Association, on 28 April 1915 with the following announcement:

LONDON, Wednesday

A supplement to the *London Gazette* issued tonight, states that the King has been pleased to approve the grant of the Victoria Cross to the undermentioned:

Private William Buckingham, 6276 Second Battalion, the Leicestershire Regiment "for conspicuous acts of bravery and devotion to duty in rescuing and rendering aid to the wounded whilst exposed to heavy fire, especially at Neuve Chapelle on the 10th and 12th March."

The news of Private Buckingham's ultimate award for gallantry came via the Superintendent's morning newspaper on 29 April. William Harrison, having read the *London Gazette* announcement and citation, went immediately to his guest and former charge and asked him to confirm his Army number. When the reply "No 6276 sir" was received William Buckingham learned, for the first time, that he had been awarded the Victoria Cross by approval of King George V.

2
FOR KING AND COUNTRY

The news that an old boy had won the Victoria Cross swept around the Countesthorpe Cottage Homes like wildfire. Private Buckingham had become a well known figure, during the previous three weeks, whilst staying there to recover from his wounds. The boys were delirious with excitement and ran around passing on the news to everyone they met. A flag was flown from the flagstaff in front of the Superintendent and Matron's residence. Private Buckingham, who had almost recovered from his injuries, was staggered by the announcement and had to prepare himself to meet representatives from the press, both locally and nationally, who were anxious to report his story.

Whilst being interviewed by a reporter from the *Daily Mail*, he was handed a telegram from the Mayor of Leicester, Alderman Jonathan North which read:

April 29th 1915
To William Buckingham,
Poor Law Offices,
Pocklington's Walk, Leicester

Hearty congratulations from the Mayor of Leicester on the noble and heroic conduct which has gained for you the proud distinction of the Victoria Cross.

Buckingham, a shy modest man, found it difficult to cope with all the adulation, and relied heavily upon the Superintendent, William Harrison, to assist him in answering the many questions put to him by reporters and journalists. Naturally, the staff at the Cottage Homes were delighted and proud of his achievements, none more so than William and Sarah Harrison who were elated at their old boy's gallantry and the

Private William Buckingham, VC walking with some of the boys on the drive at the Cottage Homes. (RECORD OFFICE FOR LEICESTERSHIRE, LEICESTER & RUTLAND)

The Poor Law Offices, Pocklington's Walk, Leicester (built 1883). (Now the offices of the Leicestershire Registration Service).
(DEREK SEATON)

Barrack block at the Regimental Depot, Glen Parva.
(DEREK SEATON)

honour that his award had brought to that tiny corner of Leicestershire. They remembered him well as a young boy: "One of the nicest lads we have ever had" was one of the comments made by Mrs Harrison to the *Leicester Daily Mercury*. She went on to say: "I would not describe him as being an angel, for he had a strong will of his own and strong-willed people occasionally come into contact with authority, but we have very pleasant memories of him." William Harrison proceeded to drive Private Buckingham to meet Walter Smith, the Chairman of the Board of Guardians, and other members of the Board gathered to greet him in Leicester. A celebratory holiday for the children, at the Cottage Homes, was discussed and it was agreed this would be arranged.

The following week Private Buckingham returned to barracks at Glen Parva. As the first soldier serving in the Leicestershire Regiment to be awarded the Victoria Cross, in the First World War, he was the hero of his Battalion and his Regiment.

He was only the second Tiger to be awarded the Victoria Cross. The first to win the VC was Corporal Philip Smith, 17th Regiment of Foot (the Leicestershire Regiment) on 18 June 1855, at the Great Redan, in the Crimean War (*London Gazette* 24 February 1857).

On 1 May, Private Buckingham received a letter from his Commanding Officer, Lieutenant-Colonel Herbert Gordon, DSO which read:

1 May 1915
Private Buckingham, VC

I am glad to send you my heartiest congratulations on being awarded the Victoria Cross by the King.

I, as your Commanding Officer, know how thoroughly you deserve the honour for on many occasions you have shown the greatest coolness and gallantry. All the Regiment are very proud of you and especially the officers.

I hope your wound will soon be healed and that you are not suffering too much pain.

8 NCOs and men besides have won the Distinguished Conduct Medal.

I hope you will soon be out again as well as ever you were.
I am,
Your well wisher,
H. Gordon.
Lieutenant-Colonel

The official notification of Private Buckingham's award appeared in Battalion Orders with the following brief entry:

Battalion Orders by
Lieutenant-Colonel H. Gordon, DSO.
Commanding 2nd Leicestershire Regiment
In the Field   19 May 1915

<u>Reward</u>   His Majesty The King has been graciously pleased to confer the Victoria Cross on No 6276 Private W.H. Buckingham, A Company.

Mention was also made of the rescue of the German soldier by Private Buckingham. The Regimental record stated that it was: "A fine instance of that Brotherhood which binds the brave of all the earth."

Private Buckingham also received a letter from Captain Cuthbert Augustine Edward Chudleigh, A Company, congratulating him upon his award in which he referred to his: "Continuous display of pluck and endurance under any circumstances day and night." Captain Chudleigh was in London recovering from a wound which had paralysed his right arm. He ended his letter with the remark: "I hope we shall both survive to run against one another in the Regimental Cross-Country championship once more."

One notable compliment came in a congratulatory letter from Brigadier-General C.G. Blackader, formerly the Commanding Officer of the 2nd Battalion of the Leicestershire Regiment. The Brigadier-General told Private Buckingham, in his letter, that no one deserved the honour more than he did and that: "All ranks of the old Regiment are proud of you." Brigadier-General Blackader, who was commissioned into the Regiment on 28 August 1888, was held in great esteem and was affectionately known as "Old Black."

All of this was a far cry from the horrors of the battlefield at Neuve Chapelle which Private Buckingham was reluctant to discuss. When asked by a reporter from the *Daily Mail*: "What was Neuve Chapelle like?" he replied: "If you give it its right name, you would call it Hell upon Earth. It was terrible." He could not be persuaded to comment further.

On Wednesday 2 June, Private Buckingham received a telegram informing him that he was to appear before King George V, in two days time, to be presented with the Victoria Cross. Friday 4 June 1915 was the proudest day of William Buckingham's life as he arrived at Buckingham Palace to be decorated by the King. Private Buckingham was one of two soldiers to have the Victoria Cross bestowed upon them by their sovereign that day, the other recipient being Lance-Corporal Wilfred Dolby Fuller, 1st Battalion Grenadier Guards. The young NCO also won his VC at Neuve Chapelle on 12 March 1915. Lance-Corporal Fuller, single-handedly, engaged a large party of enemy troops attempting to escape along a communication trench. He killed the leading man and captured the remainder (nearly 50 men). Private Buckingham and Lance-Corporal Fuller were warmly congratulated by the King for their gallantry at Neuve Chapelle. The King

Private Buckingham showing his Victoria Cross to William and Sarah Harrison outside Buckingham Palace.
(LEICESTER MERCURY)

pinned the Victoria Cross to their tunics and shook hands, cordially, with both men. Following the investiture Private Buckingham rejoined Mr and Mrs Harrison, who had accompanied him on his journey to London to receive his award from the King. He described the day as one that would always live in his memory.

The return of Private Buckingham to Countesthorpe that evening caused enormous excitement among all the children. Accompanied by William and Sarah Harrison, he arrived at Countesthorpe railway station at about 8.00 pm where he was welcomed by the band from the Cottage Homes, conducted by Charles Moore of South Wigston, and a Guard of Honour of 120 children was formed up to greet "their big brother." Many of the boys declared that they too wanted to join the Army and go to the Western Front. Everyone wanted to see the simple bronze medal which signified that the holder had been awarded the

most prestigious award for gallantry which the King could bestow. One small boy enquired what the King would say if he lost it!

A pleasant little ceremony took place the following day when, at the request of staff of the Homes, the Matron, Mrs Sarah Harrison presented William Buckingham, on their behalf, with a gold mounted walking stick which had been suitably inscribed. The Matron expressed her great pleasure at being asked to make the presentation: "To an old boy who, by his gallant conduct, had brought such honour upon himself and the Countesthorpe Cottage Homes." Mrs Harrison also read out the many letters of congratulations which had been received, including those from Private Buckingham's superior officers.

A copy of the *Leicester Daily Mercury* (5 June 1915) had been sent by one of the readers to William Crooks, the Member of Parliament for East Woolwich who, as a young boy, had been educated at the Poplar Poor Law School and went on to become the Chairman of the Poplar Board of Guardians. He promptly wrote to the editor, from the House of Commons, to say how proud he was of Private Buckingham and it was his hope that: "Every Poor Law Home or institution will have a framed record of him. Long may he be a memory to all the boys and girls whose lot may be hard" he added.

Private Buckingham was the centre of attraction at the Cottage Homes Annual Sports Day held on 15 July. The occasion was also considered to be appropriate for the town of Leicester to make a formal presentation to the first 'Tiger' to be awarded the Victoria Cross in the Great War. The presentation, before a gathering of members of the Leicester Board of Guardians and officials, took place in the school. The Mayor, Alderman Jonathan North said, in his speech, what a great day it was for the staff and children.

Alderman North declared: "The winning of the Victoria Cross is the highest honour which can fall to a soldier and that it should be awarded to a boy raised in the Cottage Homes was evidence of the good training youngsters received

Top left: Private Buckingham showing his VC to the boys at the Cottage Homes.

Top Right: Sitting surrounded by the boys.

Bottom left: Taking tea with the House Mothers.

Bottom right: Walking with William and Sarah Harrison and their dog.

(RECORD OFFICE FOR LEICESTERSHIRE, LEICESTER & RUTLAND)

Alderman Jonathan North.
(LEICESTER CITY COUNCIL)

Below: A notice of a Recruitment Meeting in Leicester attended by Private Buckingham, VC.
(LEICESTER MERCURY)

there and the parental and maternal instincts of the Superintendent and Matron, Mr and Mrs Harrison." Private Buckingham was presented with a War Loan Bond, valued at £100, and a purse containing ten guineas in cash. He returned his thanks by smartly saluting the Mayor. Private Buckingham later wrote to Alderman North expressing his gratitude for the gifts and went on to say: "What I owe to Mr and Mrs Harrison, the Superintendent and Matron, I cannot properly express. Had they been my own parents they could not have looked after my upbringing with greater care and more affectionate interest, and it was like going home to go there for my leave and to recover from my wounds."

Following his period of convalescence Private Buckingham returned to Glen Parva Barracks and proceeded to assist with recruiting throughout Leicestershire. He regularly appeared at "Patriotic Meetings" alongside other members of a recruiting team brought together under Colour Sergeant B. Pain in order to recruit men into the four Service Battalions of the Leicestershire Regiment. He was a popular figure and large crowds gathered to hear him speak and to get a glimpse of his Victoria Cross. Private Buckingham's 'Recruitment Speech' was written for him by Colour Sergeant Pain and it emphasised the need for "every man to do his little bit in fighting for freedom's cause."

During the summer of 1915 Private Buckingham had the opportunity to renew his acquaintance with one of the men he had carried off the battlefield at Neuve Chapelle. The reunion took place during a Saturday outing for wounded soldiers held at Coleorton Hall, near Ashby-de-la-Zouch, Leicestershire, where they were the guests of Mrs Abel Smith.

The transportation of the wounded soldiers was a large-scale operation and was undertaken by the members of the Leicestershire Automobile Club. The event marked the warm and unexpected meeting of Private William Buckingham with Corporal W. Tarry, A Company, 2nd Battalion of the Leicestershire Regiment, the first time they had met since they experienced the horrors of Neuve Chapelle. Corporal Tarry related how, on 12 March 1915, whilst he was a member of a reconnoitring party examining a disused trench, they came under very heavy enemy fire. He was shot in the right thigh and lost consciousness. Some five minutes later Private Buckingham found him and, with the assistance of an officer,

```
THINK !
ARE YOU CONTENT TO LET
YOUR CHUM FIGHT FOR YOU ?
TAKE YOUR PLACE AT HIS SIDE
AND
DO YOUR BIT.
―――――
MEET Private Buckingham, V.C.,
AT
AYLESTONE.
Junction of Richmond Rd. & Lansdowne Rd. at 7.45
Tram Terminus at 9 o'clock.
TO-NIGHT (THURSDAY)
```

Coleorton Hall, Coleorton, Leicestershire.
(DEREK SEATON)

Below: Private William Buckingham and Corporal W. Tarry at Coleorton Hall.
(LEICESTER MERCURY)

Lieutenant Bayfield, he was carried to safety. Corporal Tarry told reporters, at Coleorton Hall: "I have a high opinion of Buckingham. He is a man who knows no fear. I myself saw him look after seven wounded men, two or three on one day. He had a very dangerous job carrying orders from one company to another and we all noticed his bravery." He went on to say of Private Buckingham: "It did not matter who the wounded were, he would fetch them in. He was never afraid of going anywhere and I can give him the highest praise."

Corporal Tarry was discharged from active service on 4 June 1916 owing to the effects of the wound received at Neuve Chapelle.

On 3 October 1915 the death took place, at King George's Hospital, London, of 20532 Private Michael Lane from wounds received in action on 14 July 1915. Private Lane, aged 30 years, was one of the wounded soldiers carried off the battlefield at Neuve Chapelle by Private Buckingham. He was a native of Cork and had joined the Leicestershire Regiment when the Tigers were stationed in Ireland. Private Lane, a Company Signaller, had served in the Regiment for 14 years, which included a period in the Reserves, prior to being recalled following the outbreak of hostilities. He was wounded on five occasions. Following the rescue by Private Buckingham he was in Bootle

Hospital for nine weeks before returning to the Western Front.

Private Lane was buried with full military honours; Private Buckingham led the solemn funeral procession with the band, bearer party and firing party in attendance from Glen Parva Barracks, prior to interment in Groby Road Cemetery, Leicester.

The Leicestershire town of Hinckley honoured Private Buckingham and other heroes of the Leicestershire Regiment on Saturday 19 February 1916. They attended a Grand Reception at Trinity Hall and, although the event was marred by rain, thousands of people turned out to welcome them to Hinckley. The party consisted of Private William Buckingham VC, Lance-Corporal Thomas Newcombe DCM, and Lance-Corporal A.G. Robinson. The visit and Grand Reception was described in detail in the *Hinckley Echo* [22 February 1916]

Led by the band of the Countesthorpe Cottage Homes, the three soldiers were conveyed by car to the market place, through the streets of the town lined by crowds of local people. Upon arrival at the market place the heroes were welcomed by Councillor George Kinton, the Chairman of the Hinckley Urban District Council. He spoke of the deeds of the three men, commencing with the gallantry shown by Private Buckingham, including the rescue of the German soldier. Councillor Kinton then referred to the heroism of 8802 Lance-Corporal Thomas Newcombe who was awarded the Distinguished Conduct Medal at Richelbourg L'Avons on the night of 15 and 16 May 1915. Details of the award of the DCM to Lance-Corporal Newcombe were given in the announcement contained in the *London Gazette* on 5 August 1915:

8802   Private Newcombe T.
2nd Battalion,   5 August 1915
Leicestershire Regiment

For conspicuous gallantry on the night of 15 and 16 May 1915 near Richelbourg L'Avons. As an officer was severely wounded during a night attack about 20 yards from the German parapet, and at about 1.30 am Private Newcombe voluntarily went out under heavy fire of rifles, machine-guns, shrapnel and trench-mortar to bring him in. The officer was too badly wounded to move and Private Newcombe

The Leicestershire heroes upon their arrival at Hinckley Railway Station on 19 February 1916. Private W. Buckingham VC (front), L/Cpl T. Newcombe DCM (right rear) and L/Cpl A.G. Robinson (rear left).
(RECORD OFFICE FOR LEICESTERSHIRE, LEICESTER & RUTLAND)

remained with him all night and until he died on the evening of the 16th, doing what he could for him. He crawled back to our lines after dark exhausted with strain and exposure.
London Gazette 5 August 1915

Lance-Corporal Newcombe was also the recipient of the Russian Cross of St George.

Acknowledging the courage of 9781 Lance-Corporal A.G. Robinson, from Hinckley, who rescued a wounded Gurkha officer, under intense fire, and brought him back to the safety of the trenches, Councillor Kinton described how the Lance-Corporal was shot in both legs as he stepped back into the trench. His bravery earned him the Russian Medal of St George and secured for him one of 30 decorations awarded by Tsar Nicholas II of Russia to British soldiers following the Battle of Neuve Chapelle.

Throughout his lengthy spell at the Glen Parva Depot Private Buckingham became a very popular figure, not least for his unassuming manner and the professionalism he displayed as a regular soldier. He was much admired by his Commanding Officer, Lieutenant-Colonel John Mosse who was the Commandant of the Regimental Depot. Lieutenant-Colonel Mosse, who was commissioned into the Leicestershire Regiment on 13 August 1879, served with the Tigers for 24 years before taking retirement on 6 January 1904. He was recalled during the early stages of the war and received his appointment to command the Regimental Depot at Glen Parva.

Private Buckingham continued his duties recruiting men for the various battalions of the Leicestershire Regiment and was promoted to Lance-Corporal on 8 April 1916. Following a brief period at a training camp he relinquished his Lance-Corporal's stripe and returned to France on 13 April to report to the 6th Infantry Base Depot. On 23 April he was transferred to the 8th Entrenching Battalion and was promoted to Corporal five days later on 28 April. He rejoined his old unit, the 2nd Battalion of the Leicestershire Regiment and reverted to the rank of Lance-Corporal on 15 May. Almost immediately, he again relinquished his single stripe in order to join a draft of men being assembled to make up the strength of the 1st Battalion of the Regiment.

Upon his transfer to the 1st Battalion, Private Buckingham became orderly to Captain John Wilford Eric Mosse, the son of Lieutenant-Colonel Mosse. Following in the footsteps of his father, Captain Mosse was commissioned into the Leicestershire Regiment on 5 October 1910. He served with the 1st Battalion in Ireland from 1912 until 1914. Captain Mosse was an excellent long-distance runner and usually finished first or second in the Regimental cross-country runs. The 1st Battalion joined the British Expeditionary Force on the Western Front following the retreat from Mons in September 1914. Initially, Captain Mosse

Seated: Lance-Corporal Thomas Newcombe DCM & Russian Cross of St George. Standing: Private William H. Buckingham VC.
(RECORD OFFICE FOR LEICESTERSHIRE, LEICESTER & RUTLAND)

Following the funeral service Lieutenant-Colonel Mosse was laid to rest in Welford Road Cemetery, Leicester.

The third and final stage of the Battle of the Somme was planned to commence on 9 September. The 1st Battalion of the Leicestershire Regiment was camped in Mailly Wood and was one of four battalions – 9th (Service) Battalion, the Norfolk Regiment, 2nd Battalion The Sherwood Foresters (Nottinghamshire & Derbyshire Regiment), 9th Battalion the Suffolk Regiment and the 1st Battalion the Leicestershire Regiment which formed the 71st Infantry Brigade of the 6th Division, one of three divisions which made up the XIV Corps of the 4th Army. The Leicesters left Mailly Wood on 27 August and marched, in stages, throughout the next two weeks, arriving at the assembly area in the vicinity of Mealte on 11 September. They proceeded to occupy a line of trenches which had been captured earlier from the enemy. The War Diary of the 1st Battalion set the scene for the forthcoming battle:

"Orders were received on 14 September for the 4th Army, under the command of General Sir Henry Rawlinson to attack the German defences between the Combles Ravine and Martinpuich on 15 September with the object of seizing Flers, Gueudecourt, Lesboeufs and Morval and breaking through the enemy's system of defences." [See Appendix I]

The 6th Division, together with the Guards Division, was assigned the objective of capturing Morval and Lesboeufs.

The 1st Battalion, the Leicestershire Regiment moved into the attack position during the night of 14 September and was ready to engage the enemy by 4.30 am on 15 September. As they waited in the trenches, with the 9th (Service) Battalion of the Norfolk Regiment, they witnessed a sight totally new on the Western Front – the appearance of one of the very first tanks ever to be seen in action. On that September morning the tank manoeuvred its way on to the battlefield for the very first time. A British invention, the new weapon of war was observed and noted in the War Diary of the 1st Battalion with the following entry:

"15 September, about 5.50 am, a tank was noticed on our right moving quietly

Lt-Col John Mosse (55 years) with his wife, Mrs Catharine Mosse and their daughter Miss Sheila Mosse, together with two orderlies, and the family dogs, outside the Commandant's residence at the Regimental Depot, 1915.
(RECORD OFFICE FOR LEICESTERSHIRE, LEICESTER & RUTLAND)

was the Battalion Transport Officer prior to becoming Company Commander of A Company in March 1916.

Lieutenant-Colonel Mosse was delighted to receive the news that Private Buckingham, upon returning to France, had become orderly to his son. Sadly, however, Captain Mosse was called back to England following the sudden and unexpected death of his father at the Regimental Depot. Lieutenant-Colonel Mosse died in his quarters, having collapsed in the orderly room, at Glen Parva Barracks, on 17 June. His funeral, with full military honours, took place on 22 June. The funeral service was held at St Thomas' Church, South Wigston, which was built in 1892-93 and had served as the Garrison Church of the Leicestershire Regiment following the Boer War. The coffin, draped with the Union Jack, was borne on a gun-carriage with a firing party in attendance.

Left: St Thomas' Church, St Thomas' Road, (formerly Blaby Road), South Wigston.
(DEREK SEATON)

Right: The grave of Lt-Colonel Mosse and his wife, Catharine.
(DEREK SEATON)

up to the enemy's front-line – on arriving there he immediately opened fire with his machine-guns on the German trenches on either side. He was very heavily fired on by the enemy's machine-guns, which apparently had no effect, as he still continued his movements and firing."

The tank was one of three of the new weapons allocated to the 6th Division.

Zero hour for the infantry attack was fixed for 6.20 am with the 1st Battalion, the Leicestershire Regiment and the 9th (Service) Battalion, the Norfolk Regiment facing the north-east along the line of trenches due south from Ginchy. The fighting strength of the 1st Battalion, as it awaited the order to go into action, was 23 officers, including the Medical Officer and

Below: The area of the Somme where the 1st Battalion of the Leicestershire Regiment was engaged.
(DR CLIVE HARRISON)

the Chaplain, and 643 non-commissioned officers and men.

The attack commenced on time and the battalion encountered heavy machine-gun fire from the 9th Bavarian Infantry Regiment to whom they were directly opposed. Casualties were extremely heavy and among those killed in action, on 15 September 1916, was Private William Buckingham, VC of A Company. Typically, he fell as he advanced to the aid of wounded comrades. He had just cleared a parapet when he was hit in the thigh and head by machine-gun fire and was killed instantly.

Stiff resistance was met throughout the day and again on the following day. The battalion was unable to achieve its objective as a result of being held up by heavy machine-gun fire and shell-fire plus strong, undamaged barbed wire in the path of the advance. On 17 September Lieutenant-Colonel Reginald Henry Gillespie, the Commanding Officer, decided to evacuate the position and withdrew his severely depleted battalion in the early hours. The appalling casualty lists, during the intense period of fighting on 15 September, were recorded in the Battalion's War Diary:

15 September 1916
Officers   NCOs & Men
 3 Killed   108 Killed
 4 died of wounds 221 wounded
 7 wounded   22 missing

14   351

The bodies of many of those killed, including Private Buckingham, were never recovered from the battlefield and, like so many thousands of their comrades, were to be lost forever in the terrible carnage of The Somme. Following the withdrawal of the 1st Battalion on 17 September the total losses of the two day engagement amounted to 14 officers and 410 NCOs and men killed, wounded and missing.

The introduction of the tanks was of no assistance to the 6th Division. Two broke down immediately and never played a part in the battle. The remaining tank, observed by the 1st Battalion, had its periscope shot away and was, ultimately, riddled with armour-piercing bullets and had to withdraw from the action. Of the 49 tanks due to be deployed by the 4th Army on 15 September, 32 actually took part in the battle; the remaining 17 broke down en route to the battle area.

News of the appalling casualties caused enormous distress in Leicester and throughout the surrounding town and villages. The death of Private Buckingham was received with deep regret, particularly at the Countesthorpe Cottage Homes where the Superintendent, William Harrison, had the painful duty of informing the staff and children of the loss of their ex-boy, friend and hero. Captain Mosse, his Company Commander, officially communicated the news of his death in the following letter to Herbert Mansfield, Clerk to the Leicester Board of Guardians, which was published in the *Leicester Evening Mail* on 26 September:

20 September 1916
Dear Mr Mansfield
I am writing to tell you Private Buckingham VC, was killed in action on the morning of the 15th instant.

To the best of my knowledge he had no relatives and perhaps you would be so kind as to convey to his intimate friends my deepest sympathy in his loss.

For some time past he has been my personal orderly, whom it will be quite impossible to replace.

He fell wounded in the thigh and was killed instantly by a second bullet which hit him in the head.
Yours faithfully,
J.W.E. Mosse, Captain

His personal effects, which were subsequently forwarded to Herbert Mansfield and William Harrison, his Executors, included the undermentioned items:

Bible, Prayer Book, Chess Board, Cardboard box of Chessmen, Skill at Arms (Gold) – which denoted that he was a marksman – Skill at Arms (Service Dress), Stamp Album, History of the Leicestershire Regiment.

The items demonstrated William Buckingham's beliefs, hobbies and cultural pursuits.

Captain Mosse, who had been Mentioned in Despatches on two occasions, was awarded the Military Cross for conspicuous gallantry, at the Battle of the Somme, as an extract from his citation indicates: "Under very heavy fire from machine-guns and snipers he rallied his company and restored the situation to the left of the battalion front" [*London Gazette*, 4 October 1916] he was one of only 9 officers in the Company to survive the action. Captain Mosse was promoted Acting Major and Second in Command of the 1st Battalion, the Leicestershire Regiment on 22 September 1916.

Private Buckingham, along with many hundreds of local soldiers and sailors who had perished, was to have his name immortalised in a tangible form well before the end of the War was in sight. A temporary War Memorial, designed by Samuel Perkins Pick, a Leicester architect, and Benjamin John Fletcher, headmaster of the Municipal School of Art, The Newarke, Leicester, was erected on the east side of Leicester's Town Hall Square and unveiled by the Duke of Rutland on 28 June 1917. The *Leicester Evening Mail*, dated 28 June 1917, reported that the memorial: "Will answer admirably the purpose for which it is intended until the time arrives for a permanent memorial to be erected." At the time of the unveiling the War Memorial enshrined the names of 2,129 men from Leicester and Leicestershire who had perished in the War. As Francis Paul Armitage sombrely wrote: "The end of the War, which already had lasted nearly three years, apparently was far off – there was still plenty of space on the Memorial." (Armitage F.P; *Leicester 1914-1918* published 1933) The cost of the memorial was met from the 'Mayor's Fund for Disabled Warriors' and Alderman Jonathan North declared, at the unveiling ceremony, that a permanent War Memorial would follow in due course.

The Unveiling and Dedication of the temporary War Memorial.
(LEICESTER MERCURY)

The War Memorial, Victoria Park, Leicester.
(DEREK SEATON)

As promised Leicester's permanent War Memorial, designed by the eminent architect, Sir Edwin Lutyens was erected on Victoria Park, in the City, and was unveiled on 4 July 1925. A crowd of some 30,000 people assembled to remember the 9,348 men of all ranks from Leicester and Leicestershire who died in the Great War. The War Memorial was unveiled by two elderly ladies one of whom had lost four sons, and the other three sons in "The War to end all Wars." The names of the fallen were not added to the War Memorial but it stood in proud and sombre isolation as a reminder of the enormous sacrifice which had been made in the cause of freedom.

The previous year the Chairman of the Leicester Board of Guardians, Amos Martin, had established a fund to perpetuate the memory of Private William Buckingham. The fund was designated the Buckingham VC Memorial Fund and money was raised, by public subscription, for the benefit of children who had been "under the direct care, nurture or control of the Guardians of the Poor of the Parish of Leicester and their successors." Initially, a sum of £600 was raised for a cause which would have appealed to William Buckingham "who spent 9 happy years at the Countesthorpe Cottage Homes and never lost touch with the place he always called his home". [*Leicester Mercury* 7 June 1958]

Private Buckingham's name was, eventually, to appear on the Thiepval Memorial in France which commemorates the missing of The Somme. The 150 foot tall Thiepval Memorial, designed by Sir

The Thiepval War Memorial.
(PETER LOWE)

Edwin Lutyens, was the largest Commonwealth War Memorial in the world and contained the names of 74,000 Allied soldiers who died in the Battle of the Somme and had no known grave. The memorial was unveiled by His Royal Highness the Prince of Wales (later King Edward VIII) on Monday 1 August 1932. In the register of the Thiepval Memorial to the Missing, Private Buckingham's mother, Mrs Annie Susan Buckingham was recorded as residing at 35 York Street, Bedford.

Back at Countesthorpe a number of tokens and reminders to the memory of William Buckingham have been initiated over the years. On 8 June 1922 a memorial plaque was placed in the school together with his Victoria Cross and they were dedicated by Bishop Norman Lang, Bishop-Suffragan of Leicester (1913 until 1926). In 1966 it was decided to remove the medal and plaque and place them in the custody of the Leicester City Council's Museum Committee. As the village of Countesthorpe was developed after the Second World War, the decision was taken to name one of the new streets after Private Buckingham. Thus Buckingham Road took his name when the housing development, on the Leicester side of the village, was opened in 1961.

During 1986 two additional reminders of the Countesthorpe Cottage Homes VC holder were added to the local legacy of Private Buckingham. The village War Memorial, which was unveiled by HRH the Duke of York (later King George VI) on 21 November 1921, had been removed from its original position in the village square to be repositioned in the churchyard of St Andrew's Church in 1953. It was noticed in early 1986 that William Buckingham's name did not appear on the War Memorial and the Countesthorpe Parish Council agreed that his name should be engraved on the memorial.

A little later it was decided, by the Countesthorpe Parish Council, to further honour the memory of Private Buckingham in the form of a memorial to be positioned in Buckingham Road. A granite boulder, donated by EEC Quarries, formed the plinth for a bronze plaque to be fixed bearing his name and details of his gallantry. The Chairman of the Parish Council, Victor Sutherland, unveiled the memorial on 18 November 1986. The ceremony was attended by Eric Holmes of South Wigston who, as a young boy, was present when Private Buckingham visited Bassett Street School to show his Victoria Cross to the pupils and to bring greetings from many old

Buckingham Road, Countesthorpe.
(DEREK SEATON)

The memorial to Private Buckingham VC, Buckingham Road, Countesthorpe.
(HENRIETTA SCHULTKA)

The War Memorial beneath the East window of St Andrew's Church, Countesthorpe.
(DEREK SEATON)

New Walk Museum, (Joseph Aloysius Hansom 1837).
(DEREK SEATON)

South Wigstonians serving on the Western Front.

Responsibility for the Buckingham VC Memorial Fund eventually passed from the Board of Guardians to the Leicester City Council's newly appointed Public Assistance Committee on 5 January 1932. The aim of the trustees was to continue to help young people, who had been in the City Council care, with their education or preparation for entering upon some trade or profession.

The fund continues to be administered by the Leicester City Council and the emphasis remains upon assisting young people who have been in the care of the Social Services Department.

Private Buckingham's Victoria Cross and artefacts can be seen, today, at the Regimental Museum of the Royal Leicestershire Regiment which is located at the Leicester City Council's New Walk Museum in Leicester.

(In November 1946, in recognition of the fact that a battalion of the Leicestershire Regiment fought with distinction in every major theatre of the Second World War, King George VI paid the Regiment the great honour of making it a Royal Regiment).

The Victoria Cross, won at Neuve Chapelle, bears testimony to a soldier who can, rightly, be called a legend by all who revere the history and exploits of the Royal Leicestershire Regiment. Those who served in the Leicesters are proud to acknowledge that Private William Buckingham, of the 2nd Battalion, was one of the most gallant of The Tigers.

Private William Buckingham VC.
(JOHN TAYLOR)

THE FUSILIER

**Captain Robert Gee VC, MC,
2nd Battalion, The Royal Fusiliers.**
(ROBERT HARRISON)

In the reign of King James II, Colonel George Legge (1st Baron Dartmouth) raised, by command of His Majesty, "Our Royal Regiment of Fusiliers" on 11 June 1685. Fusilier comes from the French word *Fusil* – meaning a light musket.

3
A SOLDIER OF THE QUEEN

Robert Gee was born at 29 Metcalf Street, Leicester on 7 May 1876. His parents were Robert Gee, senior and Amy Gee (née Foulds) both of whom were framework knitters. Robert Gee, senior died on 27 November 1875, from pneumonia, at the Leicester Infirmary, aged 45 years, five months before his youngest son was born. The Gee family lived in a small four-roomed terraced house in St Margaret's Parish, the largest and poorest parish in the rapidly expanding town of Leicester.

The Gee family's roots lay in Leicestershire. Both of Robert Gee's parents came from the village of Anstey, four miles north-west of Leicester. They were married at the Episcopal Chapel of Anstey in the Parish of Thurcaston on 29 October 1854. Robert Gee, senior then aged 24 years was the son of William Gee, a framework knitter of Anstey and Amy, whose father John Foulds was a stone cutter, in the same village, was 19 years of age.

The young couple's first child, William was born in 1854 prior to the family moving to the village of Hathern, three miles north-west of Loughborough in Leicestershire. Four more children were born at Hathern – Thomas, Rebecca, Elizabeth and Amy. Thomas died in November 1861, aged 4 years and was buried at Hathern.

By the National Census of 1871 the Gee family had moved to 29 Metcalf Street, Leicester. Their tiny dwelling was situated in a street where every three or four families shared a privy and water tap in communal yards. A further 4 children were born in the town – Ella, Jane, Mary and finally, Robert.

Above: Metcalf Street, Leicester circa 1890. No 29 was practically opposite the Old White Hart Inn.
RECORD OFFICE FOR LEICESTERSHIRE, LEICESTER & RUTLAND)

Right: The Parish Church of St Mary, Anstey. The Episcopal Chapel where Robert Gee and Amy Foulds were married. The chapelry became a separate Ecclesiastical Parish in 1867.
(DEREK SEATON)

Robert Gee's mother, Amy died at the family home in Metcalf Street on 1 May 1885, from cardiac disease, aged 48 years and was interred in Welford Road Cemetery, Leicester where her husband had been buried almost ten years earlier.

For the next two years the young Robert, orphaned just before his ninth birthday, was cared for by his married sister Mrs Elizabeth (Betsy) Linney and her husband. Eventually, his sister felt unable to continue to care for him with the result that he was admitted to the Leicester Union Workhouse on 20 July 1887. Initially, he was only there for a short period of time prior to being sent, with three other children from the workhouse, to the Countesthorpe Cottage Homes.

He was admitted to the Cottage Homes on 5 August where he remained in the care of the Leicester Board of Guardians until shortly before his fourteenth birthday. During this time his sister, Betsy Linney visited him, unfailingly, every week. Transport was in the form of a brake and horses which brought relatives from Leicester to visit the children in the Cottage Homes. Robert always remained

Above: Looking towards Section P (Unconsecrated) Welford Road cemetery where Robert and Amy Gee were laid to rest. (DEREK SEATON)

Below: The Cottage Homes, a far cry from the harsh Victorian back streets of Leicester, where the young Robert Gee was cared for and educated from August 1887 to March 1890:
Clockwise from top left:
Cottage No 9. (DEREK SEATON)
Cottage No 8. (DR CLIVE HARRISON)
The Infirmary. (DR CLIVE HARRISON)
Boiler house and water-tower. (DEREK SEATON)

grateful for this act of kindness shown to him by his sister.

(The Cottage Homes continued to provide care for Leicester children in need until 1974. Nine of the original eleven cottages remain today plus the former staff residence. All are now in private ownership and have become attractive residential dwellings situated on, what is known as, The Drive. The school, infirmary, boiler house and water tower have also survived. The cottages and accompanying buildings were given Grade II listed building status on 21 September 1981).

Robert Gee was eventually discharged from the Cottage Homes on 8 March 1890 to become apprenticed to Robert Austin, a shoemaker at 15 Crown Street, Leicester. As the young apprentice, Robert Gee lived with the Austin family in their small cottage which also served as a workshop. After serving less than two years of his apprenticeship his indentures were cancelled; Robert Gee's explanation for this turn of events, some time later, makes interesting reading: "A high-spirited boy and an irritable old man failed to agree" (*Stanley Chronicle* 7 December 1918). The result was that he was readmitted to the Leicester Union Workhouse on 30 March 1892 by order of the Master, Frank Lambert.

The day after his readmission to Leicester Workhouse, Robert Gee applied for and was allowed out to seek work. Having found another opportunity he requested that the Board of Guardians advance him a sum of money to enable him to learn the craft of art metalworking. This was agreed upon as a result of which he was discharged from the Workhouse on 2 May 1892 to become apprenticed to Joseph Charles Shaw, General Smith and Ornamental Iron and Metal Worker (J. Shaw & Company) at 1A Carlton Street, Leicester. Joseph Shaw and his family resided in Lothair Road, Aylestone Park, Leicester. The Shaw family consisted of Joseph and his wife Eliza, their four single daughters and a 16 year old son Thomas. Both Joseph and Thomas Shaw were recorded in the National Census of 1891 as being blacksmiths. Again Robert Gee did not complete his apprenticeship but, on this occasion, it resulted from the firm of J. Shaw & Company closing down in 1893. Throughout his time with the small family business he enjoyed a cordial relationship with Joseph and Eliza Shaw.

It was at this point that Robert Gee, with the consent and encouragement of Mr and Mrs Shaw, decided to join the Army and become a regular soldier. He applied, initially, in April 1893 to join the 6th Dragoon Guards (Carabiniers) but the officer, who dealt with his application, recorded that he was: "Under the age, also too short at 5 feet 6¼ inches for the Dragoon Guards but is likely to make a smart soldier. Recommended to be accepted especially as he is a blacksmith by trade. He may join the 4th Hussars."

Thus on 8 April he enlisted, at Colchester, into the 4th (Queen's Own) Hussars (No: 3498) and gave a cousin, Fred Geary of Anstey, Leicestershire as his next of kin. He declared his age as 18 years whereas, at the time of his enlistment, he was aged 16 years and 11 months. Six months later on 18 October he went absent without leave and the following day he enlisted in the Royal Fusiliers (City of London Regiment) (No: 4821), at the Regimental Depot in Hounslow, under the name of Sydney Evershed. He, falsely, gave his parents' names as Arthur and Sarah Evershed residing at Albert Villas, Richmond Road, Aylestone Park, Leicester. Arthur Spokes Evershed was Secretary to the Harborough Liberal Association and had an office in Bishop Street, Leicester. He and his wife lived at Albert Villas, Wigston Road, Clarendon Park, Leicester.

A Court of Enquiry, held on 13 November 1893, determined that: "Private R. Gee has been illegally absent since watchsetting on 18 October 1893 and was declared to be a deserter" from the 4th (Queen's Own) Hussars.

On 9 December he was posted to the 2nd Battalion of the Royal Fusiliers serving in Guernsey. Ultimately, his former service with the 4th (Queen's Own) Hussars was discovered and, on 2 July 1894, he was imprisoned for 42 days for fraudulent enlistment and, thereby, forfeited all previous service with the Royal Fusiliers (256 days). Private Gee was released from custody on 13 August and returned to duty with the 2nd Battalion, Royal Fusiliers in Guernsey.

Following this inglorious commencement to his military career, Private Gee quickly made amends and went on to demonstrate his ability and determination to make a success of his chosen profession. He was promoted Lance-Corporal on 1 January 1896 and, following posting to the 1st Battalion, Royal Fusiliers, he served from 25 November 1896 to 14 March 1900 in the East Indies. Whilst in India he was promoted to Corporal on 20 August 1898. On returning to the United Kingdom he was posted to the 4th Battalion on 15 March 1900 and received further promotion to the rank of Sergeant on 1 August 1900. Sergeant Gee proved himself to be a first class all-round sportsman and he excelled at hockey and cross-country running.

Whilst he was stationed at Shorncliffe Camp, Cheriton, Kent, Sergeant Gee met Miss Elizabeth Dixon, the daughter of Peter Dixon of Huntingdon. They met at the Baptist chapel in Folkestone whilst Elizabeth was staying with her eldest sister who lived at 11 Trinity Close in the seaside resort. Elizabeth was the great-niece of John Jones of Tal-y-sarn, Caernarfon (now Gwynedd). They were married at the Salem (Baptist) church in Folkestone on 8 March 1902. Robert Gee was aged 25 years and his bride Elizabeth was 27 years of age, her father's details were recorded as being – Peter Dixon, Gardener. The couple's first child, a daughter, Edith Tannycastell Gee was born on 7 December 1902 at 103 Samuel Street, Woolwich, London SE18 where they were living in married quarters close to the Regimental Garrison of the Royal Regiment of Artillery. (The Welsh name of Tannycastell should, strictly speaking, be spelt Tan-y-castell and means "below the castle" – it is believed that the family, whose lineage has been traced back to 1170 A.D., may have had its origins "beneath the walls of Caernarfon Castle").

On 4 March 1904, Sergeant Robert Gee was promoted to Colour-Sergeant. The following year a second daughter, Amy Tannycastell Gee was born in Dublin, on 14 May 1905, her father being stationed with the 4th Battalion, Royal Fusiliers at Portobella Barracks, Dublin.

By 1907, Colour Sergeant Gee and his family were back in Southern England. A further period of service spent at the Regimental Deport at Hounslow, where the family lived in married quarters, was to prove quite decisive both in terms of advancing his military career and developing a range of interests beyond his everyday duties as a senior Non-Commissioned Officer. On 30 June 1907 he became a Freemason and was initiated into Roll Call Lodge (No 2523) then meeting at Hounslow. He was passed to the Second Degree on 13 September and raised to the Third Degree on 14 November 1907. Throughout the history of Freemasonry a great number of Military and Naval men have been Masons and many Lodges were founded specifically for members of the Armed Forces.

During 1908 he suffered with heart trouble but remained with his unit as Company Pay Sergeant, O Company, 6th Battalion at Hounslow. On 8 November 1908 he assumed the duties of Orderly Room Sergeant. Further advancement came on 1 January 1911 when he was promoted to Regimental Quartermaster-Sergeant. In November 1912 he was awarded the Long Service and Good Conduct Medal. The years leading up to the outbreak of the First World War were used, constructively, by RQMS Gee who, during this period, rigorously studied military history and was appointed a lecturer in the subject. He was, at that time, one of only a handful of NCOs deemed to be qualified to teach military history. The depot of the Royal Fusiliers, at Hounslow, was also the home of a cavalry regiment, before the war and Robert Gee took the opportunity to learn to ride for which he was required to play his part in the mucking out of the stables and the grooming of the horses.

Following the declaration of war by Great Britain on Germany, on 4 August 1914, Regimental Quartermaster-Sergeant Gee was posted to the 6th Reserve Battalion of the Royal Fusiliers which was mobilised at Hounslow, within a matter of days, and posted to the new battalion's war station at Dover. The battalion manned defensive positions and the unit formed part of the Dover defences. In addition the 6th Reserve

Battalion was fully equipped for action on the Western Front and, on occasions, the strength of the unit was in excess of 4000 officers and men, the majority of whom were recruits under training. The staff instructors consisted mainly of senior NCOs of the Royal Fusiliers who were responsible for the training and preparation of drafts for the British Expeditionary Force. During this early period of the war the Gee family moved from Hounslow to married quarters in Dover.

On 29 January 1915 RQMS Gee was promoted to Warrant-Officer, Class II (QMS). Meanwhile his parent unit, the 2nd Battalion, Royal Fusiliers, which was, by this time, part of the 86th Infantry Brigade, 29th Division was based in a transit camp at Stockingford, near Nuneaton, Warwickshire. Various battalions of the 29th Division, which was formed in January 1915, were billeted in the towns and villages in the area whilst undergoing training to prepare them for the impending campaign in the Dardenelles. On 12 March the Division, consisting of 11 regular battalions of highly professional and experienced soldiers together with one Edinburgh Territorial Force Battalion, paraded at Stretton-on-Dunsmore, Warwickshire where they were reviewed by King George V who took the salute as his troops marched past.

The 2nd Battalion entrained for Avonmouth on 15 March from where they sailed for Egypt and disembarked at Alexandria on 29 March. Four weeks later the Dardenelles Expeditionary Force, commanded by General Sir Ian Hamilton, arrived off Gallipoli. The object of the campaign, which commenced on 25 April, was to take the Gallipoli Peninsula, capture Constantinople and force Germany's ally Turkey out of the war, whilst at the same time giving Russia command of the Black Sea. (See Appendix II). During the first four months of the ill-fated attack at Gallipoli the 2nd Battalion suffered very heavy casualties as they fought to penetrate strongly held Turkish positions in the ridges and hills overlooking Cape Helles. The ranks of the battalion were decimated beyond recognition and had to be practically rebuilt to achieve effective fighting strength.

The role of the long serving senior NCOs was all important in the crucial task of rebuilding the depleted units. Warrant Officer Gee, who had remained as an instructor with the 6th Reserve Battalion at Dover, was commissioned into the 2nd Battalion, Royal Fusiliers on 21 May 1915 having served in the ranks for 21 years and 165 days, including 113 days as a Warrant Officer, Class II (29 January to 20 May 1915).

4
COMRADES IN ARMS

Second-Lieutenant Robert Gee arrived in Gallipoli on 5 September to find that his battalion had been relieved and withdrawn from the front line four days earlier. The War Diary of the 2nd Battalion, dated 8 September 1915, recorded the casualties sustained since the landing at Cape Helles on 25 April:

Killed	279
Wounded	954
Missing	103
Sick	400

Of the original personnel of the 2nd Battalion, who arrived at Gallipoli four and a half months earlier, there was not one single officer remaining and only 166 other ranks had survived. Second-Lieutenant Gee was appointed a Company Commander upon his arrival and by 11 September he was deployed in giving daily lectures to his men. The 2nd Battalion having been rebuilt to effective fighting strength then sailed, on 21 September, in HMS *Princess* for Suvla Bay, situated to the north-west of the Gallipoli Peninsula. They immediately moved into the front line to relieve the South Wales Borderers and, on 27 September, Second-Lieutenant Gee was promoted Acting Captain. For the next two months the 2nd Battalion was regularly involved in action.

On 26 November the Royal Fusiliers were, once again, subjected to the unimaginable horrors of war. The events of that fateful night were recorded in a lengthy and detailed account in the 2nd Battalion's War Diary and in an article (No 363) written by Captain Gee which was subsequently published in the series "*I Was There*" by the Waverley Book Company in the 1930s.

Captain Gee recorded that in the early evening: "A terrible clap of thunder, worse than a bombardment of high explosive, broke the stillness of the night. This was followed by zigzags of lightning which appeared to split the heavens in two and the rain fell as only it can fall in the tropics. Within half an hour the trenches held a foot of water, rushing so quickly it

Exhausted men of the 2nd Battalion, Royal Fusiliers resting in the trenches.
(THE ROYAL FUSILIERS MUSEUM)

was difficult to stand. At 7.00 pm the barricade gave way and a solid wall of water seven feet high swept into the trench carrying everything and everybody before it."

The account in the War Diary read: "A tremendous flood of water then poured into our trenches drowning several men. A mule, a pony and 3 dead Turks were actually brought into the trench by the water. In the space of 2 minutes our entire sector was converted into a regular lake."

By 8.00 pm the situation had eased slightly and Captain Gee was able to swim from a tree to reach some of his men trapped in a trench where the water-level was chest high. Elsewhere trenches had been washed away burying men in the mud. As the night wore on the temperature dropped dramatically and there was a severe frost followed by snow of blizzard proportions.

The War Diary recorded that men who survived were all soaked to the skin, added to which many had lost their rifles and greatcoats. Those men who managed to scramble out of the waterlogged trenches, on to the higher ground, found themselves in dangerously exposed positions and many were killed by Turkish sniper fire. Many who had survived drowning, died from exposure and frost-bite.

The horrors of Suvla Bay increased in magnitude and were vividly described in Captain Gee's report of the incident:

"With the help of the sergeant-major, I counted the company, and of the 139 only 69 remained. It was soon discovered that the ration party had been drowned, and all the food and drink we had was one gallon jar of rum. This was issued out and Private Oldfield, who had swum to headquarters, brought up orders that the line was to be held at all costs. This order was also brought to me by the adjutant.

"All day the weather was freezing and more men died. Towards night it turned to rain and it was impossible to move. At 2.00 am, 28th, the commanding officer brought me half a bottle of whisky and told me that the adjutant and himself were the only living persons at the battalion headquarters."

By 3.30 am all of Captain Gee's officers and most of the NCOs had perished and, after releasing those men no longer able to fight, to make their way back to a dressing station, he counted up the remainder and found: "I had only 27 living souls in the firing line and only ten rifles in working order." Following further heavy rain and frost the order came, at 5.30 am, on 28 November to "withdraw and retire to brigade headquarters." Captain Gee stayed with the last four men and, whilst withdrawing under heavy fire, all four of his men were killed, the last man dying in his arms.

The following day the War Diary recorded:

"29 November
Freezing hard, strength of Battalion (4.00 pm) 105 men – 31 in a state of collapse, and 11 officers."

On 30 November, Lieutenant-General Sir Julian Byng, the Corps Commander of IV Corps at Suvla Bay inspected the depleted 2nd Battalion. The War Diary, for the day, stated that at the 4.00 pm roll call 10 officers and 84 remained of which 70 were effective from an original battalion strength of 22 officers and 661 NCOs and men. Captain Gee, as Company Commander of W Company, was to record that, from a company strength of 139:

"Poor W Company mustered two, Sergeant-Major Pascall and myself."

(9972 Company Sergeant-Major Frederick W. Pascall was an Acting Warrant Officer, Class II)

At the time of the great flood and blizzard at Suvla Bay, and the resultant physical and psychological stress borne by the Royal Fusiliers, in the front line, Captain Gee was 39 years of age.

The battalion withdrew in stages, from the forward area, and embarked from W Beach, on a trawler, for Cape Helles on 16 December. By early December Lieutenant-General Byng had recommended the closure of the Gallipoli campaign and had drawn up plans for the successful evacuation of the Allied Forces. On 5 January 1916 the remnants of the 2nd Battalion finally sailed for Egypt, on SS *Caledonia*, where they disembarked two days later at Alexandria. The evacuation of Gallipoli was completed at 4.00 am on 9 January 1916, it was a skilful and well-planned withdrawal with no Allied losses – not a single life was lost.

Following the movement of the 2nd Battalion to Egypt, Captain Gee was appointed Acting Staff Captain at Headquarters, 86th Brigade, on 2 February. Meanwhile, his battalion moved to Suez, to occupy an old Army camp, on 4 March. Further promotion quickly followed when he took over the post of Staff Captain at Brigade Headquarters, on 13 March, after serving in the post, in a temporary capacity, for only five weeks. The following day the 86th Brigade began to embark for the Western Front. The brigade, which included the 2nd Battalion, the Royal Fusiliers, left Port Tewfik for France, on 14 March, on board the SS *Alunia*, with a complement of 31 officers and 910 other ranks.

Acting Captain Gee, technically still in the rank of Second-Lieutenant, was promoted to Lieutenant on 21 March. He was soon back in the front line with the 2nd Battalion, (whilst retaining his appointment as Staff Captain with the 86th Infantry Brigade), as final preparations were made for the commencement of the Battle of the Somme. On that fateful day, 1 July 1916 the 2nd Battalion, Royal Fusiliers went into action near Beaumont Hamel. Captain Gee was seriously wounded in the engagement whilst showing distinguished leadership, and was carried from the battlefield in a semi-conscious condition. On 4 July, suffering from a wound in the thigh and from shell-shock, he was evacuated to England with many wounded comrades on the *St David*, arriving at Southampton. After medical treatment he went on sick leave to be with his family at 20 St Andrew's Terrace, Dover. The gallantry displayed by Captain Gee did not go unnoticed by his superior officers and, in the *London Gazette* (22 September 1916), it was announced that he had been awarded the Military Cross. The citation which confirmed the award to Captain Gee for his actions on 1 July, the first day of the Battle of the Somme, read as follows:

> Second Lieutenant (temporary Captain) Robert Gee, Royal Fusiliers. He encouraged his men during the attack by fearlessly exposing himself and cheering them on. When wounded he refused to retire and urged his men on till, after being blown in the air by a shell, he was carried in half-unconscious.

Captain Gee was also Mentioned in Despatches, during September, for his part in an earlier action on the Western Front. He remained on sick leave until 19 October and, during this period of convalescence, he spent his time learning French. He also renewed his Freemasonry connections and was appointed Senior Warden on 12 October.

Following his recovery, Captain Gee returned to France in February 1917 where he served as a Staff Captain with the redoubtable 29th Division until 24 June. The following day he returned to his former appointment as a Staff Captain with the 86th Infantry Brigade. Shortly afterwards, on 13 August, he was wounded again and received treatment at a dressing station at the 88th Field Ambulance prior to returning to his brigade on 31 August.

During the autumn of 1917, HRH the Prince of Wales (later Edward VIII) made one of his many visits to the rear areas of the front lines. On one of these occasions Captain Gee was appointed Temporary ADC to the Prince. They were together for only a day or so but their meeting left a lasting impression with Captain Gee, who held the Prince in high esteem.

The 86th Brigade was, by this time, continually in action at the Ypres Salient where, once again, Captain Gee rose to the occasion in meeting a rather unusual demand thrust upon him in his role as a Staff Captain. On 11 October the brigade was relieved at Elverdinghe whereupon the Brigade Commander, Brigadier-General George Ronald Hamilton Cheape ordered Captain Gee to return to Headquarters to prepare a hot meal for the exhausted men. The Staff Captain responded by organising "a savoury and appetising stew" for the men of his brigade upon their marched return to a point known as Crocodile Pontoon. Some months later Brigadier-General Cheape enquired of Captain Gee how he managed to obtain such a plentiful supply of fresh meat at a moment's notice. He was duly informed that his Staff Captain, together with an orderly, had used meat from the carcasses of a team of mules which had been killed by enemy shell-fire! This incident was duly recorded in *The Story of the 29th Division* by Captain Stair Gillon.

By mid-October the Third Battle of Ypres had become completely bogged down in the mud of Passchendaele whereupon a plan to mount a new offensive at Cambrai, to the south-east, was agreed by the British Commander-in-Chief, Field Marshal Sir Douglas Haig (See Appendix I). This was to be the first battle in which a massed attack by tanks was mounted as part of the 3rd Army, under its newly-promoted Commander, General Sir Julian Byng. A contingent of 378 fighting tanks plus some 50 supply tanks was used in the offensive.

The attack commenced on 20 November and two corps were deployed. The III Corps, which was comprised of 4 divisions, including the 29th Division, attacked on the right supported by two Tank Brigades. The initial progress of III Corps was highly successful but was soon slowed down with heavy casualties being taken which resulted in the British High Command closing down the offensive on 27 November. By 29 November a German counter-attack was imminent and the enemy assault commenced the following day.

The 86th Brigade was positioned beyond the St Quentin Canal as part of the 29th Division's frontal force. The 2nd Battalion, Royal Fusiliers had returned two days earlier as a counter-attack battalion and, as the German infantry made rapid progress, the Brigade Commander, Brigadier-General George Cheape sent his Staff Captain, Captain Robert Gee to inform the 87th Brigade of the deteriorating situation and to request assistance. He was also ordered to warn a detachment of sappers, of the Royal Engineers, in the village of Les Rues Vertes which was in danger of being taken by the enemy, thus cutting off British troops located in the twin village of Masnieres on the other side of the St Quentin Canal.

Two companies of the 2nd Battalion, Royal Fusiliers were ordered across the canal to form a defensive flank at the former headquarters of the 86th Brigade in the village of Les Rues Vertes. Almost immediately, upon arrival, two platoons were engaged in street fighting with the enemy who had already captured the ammunition dump located in the village. By 8.50 am it appeared that the village had virtually been lost. It was from this point onwards that Captain Gee proceeded to display leadership and heroism of the highest order.

He was ordered to establish a defensive flank, his small force consisting of Captain Loseby of the 1st Battalion, Lancashire Fusiliers and 12 men. Captain Gee sent the officer and 6 of the men – 4 signallers and 2 orderlies – to make contact with the 16th Battalion, the Duke of Cambridge's Own (the Middlesex Regiment), at the lock bridge, whilst he and the remainder of his small party prepared to engage the enemy. Within minutes Captain Gee and four of his men were firing upon the advancing German soldiers whilst the other two men quickly built a barricade using tables, chairs and anything they could lay their hands on. The enemy was kept at bay for some five minutes whilst a Lewis gun was brought up in support.

Captain Gee then decided he must reach the brigade ammunition dump which was located in the second house beyond the barricade. With great determination he knocked a hole through the wall of the house and crawled through to the ammunition store where he was seized by two German guards. His period of captivity lasted only for a matter of minutes during which, in a violent struggle, he killed one of his captors with his spiked stick whilst the other was shot by his orderly.

Having returned to the street Captain Gee took command of 30 to 40 men of the Guernsey Light Infantry who had arrived to give support. Some were despatched to assist Captain Loseby and his force whilst the remainder were deployed in erecting another barricade. Meanwhile, Captain

An Artist's impression, which appeared in The War Illustrated, *dated 5th January 1918, showing Captain Robert Gee in action immediately prior to his escape.*

Gee and his original party of 6 men secured the bomb store and cleared the houses. By this time two companies of Guernsey Light Infantry had arrived, so enabling Captain Gee to take command of a larger force of men.

He then established a bombing party which speedily cleared the houses along the Marcoing Road resulting in the enemy being driven to the southern edge of the village. Having succeeded thus far, Captain Gee then concentrated upon supplying ammunition to the troops on the other side of the canal and those located at the bridges.

Assessing the overall situation from the château, Captain Gee observed that the enemy was digging in some 100 yards to the south-west of the village with a machine-gun being mounted. He ordered a Stokes gun to be brought up and, whilst this was being fired, he and an orderly rushed the machine-gun post. The orderly was shot but Captain Gee reached his objective and, with his two revolvers, he shot the eight Germans and captured the gun. The machine gun was then used against the enemy infantry when observed advancing in the direction of the village.

The official report of the action is graphically chronicled in the recommendation signed by Captain Gee's superior officers:

86th Brigade 29th Division III Corps
9-12-17 Date of recommendation
Action for which commended
Honour or reward: V.C.
For conspicuous bravery at MASNIERES and LES RUES VERTES on November 30th 1917. A surprise attack by a large German force having pierced our line south of the front held by this Division the enemy penetrated LES RUES VERTES capturing our rear Brigade Headquarters and Ammunition Dump.

Captain Gee, finding himself a prisoner, killed a German with his broken stick, escaped, and organised a party of the Brigade Staff with which he attacked the enemy fiercely. He was closely followed by two companies of infantry, who mopped up for him. By his own personal bravery and prompt action he and his orderlies cleared the streets. He established a defensive flank on the outskirts of the village with the exception of a post held by a German machine gun. Captain Gee, followed by one man, rushed the gun, a revolver in each hand, killed eight men of the crew and captured the gun. This gun was then turned on the enemy's infantry and guns which were seen advancing on MARCOING. At this time he was wounded but made certain that the defence was organised before he would even have the wound dressed.

During the day he had five orderlies shot by his side,

His magnificent exploit saved the Brigade if not the Division.

Signed by G R H Cheape, Brigadier-General commanding the 86th Infantry Brigade and by Sir Beauvoir de Lisle, Major-General commanding the 29th Division

The report was then forwarded to Lieutenant-General Sir William Pulteney commanding the III Corps and upwards, through the chain of command, for final approval for the award of the Victoria Cross by the King.

Following the action, Captain Gee, reluctantly, retired back to a dressing station of the 37th Field Ambulance, on 1 December, to have a gunshot wound to his right knee treated and dressed. At 7.00 pm on 1 December orders were received for the evacuation of Masnieres and Les Rues Vertes.

Meanwhile Captain Gee was again Mentioned in Despatches on 11 December for his involvement in an earlier action. Eight days later, after spending less than three weeks at the dressing station he returned to duty on 19 December. He was Mentioned in Despatches for the third time during January 1918.

Ultimately the award of the Victoria Cross to Captain Gee was confirmed. The announcement and citation appeared in the *London Gazette* on 11 January 1918.

At the time of the announcement he was 41 years of age – twice the age of some of the young soldiers under his command. His skilled and forceful leadership, together with his acts of gallantry, resulted in young men, in the ranks, responding, instantly, to the orders of an experienced older officer who always led by example.

An interesting anecdote relates to the sword which Captain Gee possessed. It was actually a sabre which belonged to Major (later Lieutenant-Colonel) Septimus Frederick Legge who was commissioned into the 1st (King's) Dragoon Guards on 10 November 1888 and subsequently transferred to the Royal Fusiliers on 23 April 1892. Major Legge gave his sabre to Captain Gee to look after it for him until the end of the war. The Major retired from the Army in 1917 but the sabre remained in the care of Captain Gee. The irony of becoming the custodian of a sabre, which was the property of a former officer in the Dragoon Guards would not have been lost on Captain Gee who, as an under-age recruit had, in 1893, unsuccessfully applied to join the 6th Dragoon Guards (Carabiniers)!

Whilst back in England, in early 1918, Captain Gee received the following telegram:

19 February 1918

Telegram from Lord Chamberlain

Your attendance is required at Buckingham Palace on Saturday next the Twenty-third instant at 10 o'clock AM.
Service Dress. Please telegraph acknowledgement.
Lord Chamberlain, London

On 23 February Captain Robert Gee, accompanied by his younger daughter Amy, aged 12 years, was decorated with the Victoria Cross by King George V at Buckingham Palace

He was soon back in France once more and, shortly after arriving again on the Western Front, he was admitted to a divisional rest station of the 89th Field Ambulance on 5 April suffering with gastritis. Following treatment he was

Left: Captain Robert Gee, VC, MC, leaving Buckingham Palace after receiving his Victoria Cross from King George V.
(PHOTOGRAPH COURTESY OF THE IMPERIAL WAR MUSUEM, LONDON. Q80673)

gave Captain Gee greater feelings of pride than the events of Thursday 11 July when, together with his wife and elder daughter Edith, aged 15 years, he arrived back in his native Leicester to be accorded a Civic welcome. He was met at London Road railway station by Walter Carver the Chairman of the Leicester Board of Guardians and a large gathering of well-wishers. Having inspected a Guard of Honour a procession was formed, headed by the Countesthorpe Cottage Homes' and the Cadets' Band to accompany Captain Gee to the Town Hall. He was introduced, on the steps of the Town Hall, to Alderman Jonathan North, the Mayor of Leicester who had been a member of the Leicester Board of Guardians during the time when the young Robert Gee was in the care of the Countesthorpe Cottage Homes.

Alderman North extended a very warm welcome to Captain Gee and his family, and read out a letter he had received from William Crooks, Member of Parliament for Woolwich, who asked: "Will you please add my congratulations on the glorious honour Captain Gee had brought to the schools at Countesthorpe. As an old boy of one myself I wish him long life and happiness." It was William Crooks, MP who had, so generously, paid similar compliments and good wishes to Private William Buckingham in 1915.

The Mayor then presented Captain Gee with a gold watch and chain which evacuated to England, three days later, on 8 April.

Messages of congratulations, upon his award of the Victoria Cross, were received by Captain Gee from many quarters, including a congratulatory telegram from the Prince of Wales who reminded him of a pair of red socks which Captain Gee had worn whilst acting as temporary ADC to the Prince on the Western Front!

Of the many accolades received, none

Below: The Town Hall, Leicester (Francis Hames 1876).
(DEREK SEATON)

had been subscribed to by his friends and admirers in Leicester. The watch was inscribed: "Presented to Captain Gee, VC, MC, on the occasion of his public reception by the Mayor and citizens of the Borough of Leicester, 11 July 1918." A gold brooch was presented to Mrs Gee and Alderman North said he was sure: "They would treasure the gifts to remind them of this auspicious occasion."

The hero of the hour responded by expressing his gratitude for the recognition by his home town. He informed the gathering: "The world knows nothing of the greatest heroes" and declared that: "Every recipient of the Victoria Cross was always ready to admit that he was lucky he happened to be in the limelight and that others more deserved the coveted distinction." He recalled the intense fighting on November 1917: "When thousands of fellow soldiers earned the VC but very few were given." [*Leicester Mercury* 11 July 1918]

In the afternoon Captain Gee visited the Countesthorpe Cottage Homes, with his wife and daughter, on the occasion of the Annual Sports Day. He was given a tremendous reception to mark the return of the second old boy, from the homes, to be awarded the Victoria Cross. For the children who had welcomed back Private William Buckingham in 1915, following his investiture at Buckingham Palace, to be able to experience such excitement for a second time was an event they would never forget. Captain Gee made himself thoroughly at home and was especially popular among the boys.

Members of staff were equally pleased to welcome him, none more so than the Superintendent and Matron, William and Sarah Harrison. Sadly, they had lost their elder son, Private (41591) Norman Cyril John Harrison of the Manchester Regiment who died of gas-poisoning at Ypres, on 13 June 1917, aged 20 years. On a happier note, the occasion marked the meeting of the Harrisons' younger son Douglas (18 years) with Captain and Mrs Gee's elder daughter Edith (15 years). This chance meeting was to lead to a

Captain Gee showing his Victoria Cross to a group of young boys at the Countesthorpe Cottage Homes.
(RECORD OFFICE FOR LEICESTERSHIRE, LEICESTER & RUTLAND)

Wellington Barracks, Birdcage Walk, London SW1. (DEREK SEATON)

Westminster Abbey Looking towards the West Front Entrance. (DEREK SEATON)

John Williams, 2nd Battalion, 24th Foot (later The South Wales Borderers) who won his Victoria Cross at Rourkes Drift, Natal on 23 January 1879 (*London Gazette* 2 May 1879). The queue that formed for his autograph was a remarkable tribute to one of only two survivors, in 1920, of one of the greatest epics in the annals of British military history.

A far more sombre occasion took place on Armistice Day, 11 November 1920, when the King unveiled the Cenotaph in Whitehall followed by the interment of the body of the Unknown Warrior in Westminster Abbey. A Guard of Honour, one hundred strong, was comprised of 71 holders of the Victoria Cross plus 29 officers and men who had otherwise distinguished themselves, during the First World War, by winning awards for gallantry. In a number of instances officers, (including Captain Gee), and men, had been awarded more than one decoration for gallantry.

The Army recipients assembled on the main parade ground at Chelsea Barracks at 8.30 am. "By his Majesty's wish they will be sized irrespective of rank and will march with the VC guard of the Royal Navy and the Royal Air Force to Westminster Abbey arriving at the Great North Gate by 10.00." [*The Times* 11 November 1920]

Following the unveiling of the Cenotaph by the King, the gun-carriage, drawn by six horses, bearing the body of the Unknown Warrior proceeded slowly to Westminster Abbey followed by King George V, as chief mourner, the Royal Princes, the Prime Minister, David Lloyd George and the Ministers of State. The gun-carriage was met at Westminster Abbey by the clergy following which the coffin of the Unknown Warrior passed slowly through the Guard of Honour drawn up in two lines, without distinction of rank, under the command of Lieutenant-Colonel Bernard Cyril Freyberg, VC, DSO and three bars, 1st Battalion, the Grenadier Guards. "Never has a warrior before had such a Guard of Honour." [*The Times* 12 November 1920]

Early in 1921 Captain Gee was given a further opportunity to gain a seat in the House of Commons. The *Woolwich Gazette and Plumstead News* announced, on 15 February, that the right Honourable William Crooks, Member of Parliament for East Woolwich, had decided to give up his seat with immediate effect owing to serious ill-health. Will Crooks, as he was affectionately known, was a popular MP who had represented Woolwich in the House of Commons from 1903 to January 1910 and again from December 1910 onwards. He was the Member of Parliament who had written to both Private Buckingham (1915) and Captain Gee (1918) to personally congratulate them upon being awarded the Victoria Cross.

Two candidates quickly emerged to contest the by-election in East Woolwich. Captain Gee was selected as the Coalition Unionist representative whilst James Ramsay MacDonald was chosen as the Labour candidate. Ramsay MacDonald had struggled to come to terms with his defeat in Leicester in 1918 and had hoped to return to Westminster via Aberavon in South Wales where he had been chosen as the prospective candidate. When the opportunity presented itself in East Woolwich he was persuaded, after some initial hesitancy, to contest the by-election. Nominations took place at Woolwich Town Hall on 21 February and the date was fixed for Wednesday 2 March.

Thus the stage was set for a political battle, of some magnitude, between a Leicester born lad Robert Gee and a former Member of Parliament for Leicester, Ramsay MacDonald.

The electorate of East Woolwich was 33,444 in total of which almost a third were employed at the Royal Arsenal, Woolwich. Many were on short-time, following their tremendous efforts, to keep up the supplies of munitions, during the war years. Also included were 13,837 women who were eligible to vote for the very first time in East Woolwich. (It was not possible for them to vote in the 1918 General Election owing to William Crooks being returned unopposed). The local newspapers gave wide coverage of the two candidates in the forthcoming "Woolwich Battle." One headline read:

VC v Pacifist

Captain Gee declared: "Probably I know more than anybody today about the hardships of the working classes, and I can speak for them as authoritatively as any theoretical Labour leader in the House of Commons. I have worked with my hands all my life. I started life as a workhouse boy, spending three years in a home, and so I consider myself more entitled to speak for working people than almost anybody today." Certainly Captain Gee knew the East Woolwich constituency well having lived in Samuel Street, in the Borough, some twenty years earlier. The short campaign proved to be an acrimonious affair with

Woolwich Town Hall, London SE18.
(DEREK SEATON)

huge crowds attending the meetings of both candidates and the police being kept at full stretch to combat hostile elements bent on physical exchanges.

Ramsay MacDonald was able to draw upon his considerable experience as a Member of Parliament and his leadership of the Labour Party (1911-1914). Against this, his opposition to the First World War and, what was perceived by some, as his 'pacifist' tendencies caused doubts in the minds of many of the electorate. Captain Gee, on the other hand, was clearly admired by many as a hero, with an outstanding wartime record, who was prepared to fight for the retention of the Woolwich Arsenal, albeit at reduced manning levels.

During the campaign Captain Gee was, briefly, back in Leicestershire where he was the guest of William Lindsay Everard at his home at Ratcliffe Hall, Ratcliffe-on-the-Wreake. On 19 February Captain Gee unveiled a War Memorial in the form of a tablet in Swithland slate, inserted in the wall of St Botolph, the village church, in memory of the men from the tiny community who died in the First World War. From a population of just over 100 people, 20 men were sent to serve their King and Country. During the conflict two were killed, five were wounded and, incredibly, three were awarded the Military Medal. [*Leicester Mercury* 21 February 1921]

On 24 February, Horatio William Bottomley the Unionist MP for South Hackney was due to address a meeting, at Plumstead Baths, on behalf of Captain Gee. A hostile crowd of some 2,000 people gathered outside the baths and, despite a considerable police presence, it was not possible for Horatio Bottomley to enter the building. He was escorted to Plumstead Police Station, for his own protection. Meanwhile Captain Gee was fully engaged in a lively meeting in the baths. At one stage, in the proceedings, a heckler shouted: "Don't vote for him. He's a bastard!" Taking this to be a reference to the fact that his father died before he was born, Captain Gee leapt from the stage to confront the heckler, in the process he tripped and fell and injured his right arm. Upon leaving the Plumstead Baths it was alleged that

The Church of St Botolph, Ratcliffe-on-the-Wreake Leics.
(DEREK SEATON)

The Swithland slate tablet unveiled by Captain Robert Gee, VC, MC.
(DEREK SEATON)

Captain Gee was struck over the head by a woman armed with a chair-leg. The following day he was unable to attend a meeting, due to be held at Church Manorway School, Plumstead, as it was said that he was confined to his bed, the injury sustained having affected his old war wound to the head. None of these events were helpful to Ramsay MacDonald, who strenuously denied that any hooliganism and loutish behaviour could in anyway be associated with the Labour Party. Sympathy and increased support were shown for Captain Gee which, together with his articulate and persuasive campaigning, indicated that the result of the by-election was going to be extremely close.

5
SOLDIER TO POLITICIAN

The declaration of the East Woolwich by-election was announced, after a recount, at Woolwich Town Hall:

Captain Robert Gee, VC, MC
(Coalition Unionist) 13,724
James Ramsay MacDonald
(Labour) 13,041
Coalition majority 683

East Woolwich had made its choice, Captain Robert Gee was elected to Parliament and Ramsay MacDonald was again consigned to the political wilderness.

Within days of becoming a Member of Parliament, Captain Gee and his wife attended the Melton Hunt Steeplechases at Burton Lazars, Leicestershire where they were given a very warm welcome.

On Saturday 5 March, Captain Gee and Sir Kingsley Wood, the Coalition Unionist MP for West Woolwich were entertained to breakfast by the Prime Minister, David Lloyd George who warmly congratulated the victor upon a notable triumph and Sir Kingsley Wood upon the manner he had conducted the election campaign. The event was reported fully in the *Woolwich Gazette & Plumstead News* of 8 March and Captain Gee, when asked for his impressions, after the breakfast, said: "It was certainly one of the proudest moments of my life. I little thought, when a workhouse boy, that I should ever be the guest of the Prime Minister of Great Britain. I was very glad to be able to thank Mr Lloyd George for all he did during the Great War for my fighting pals."

Captain Gee then took his seat in the House of Commons on Monday 7 March 1921.

The new MP for East Woolwich received 213 telegrams and over 500 letters, including many from comrades in his old regiment, congratulating him upon his success. He quickly settled into the life of a Member of Parliament and attended the House of Commons on a regular basis; he was not averse to late night sittings but was often obliged to leave the chamber due to the effects of his war wounds. He often spoke on a number of issues which were important to him, particularly on military matters including Army estimates and questions relating to ex-servicemen. He worked to secure better pensions especially for those who had been gassed and to obtain financial assistance for war widows. Captain Gee spoke passionately on these matters and, in doing so, displayed his unmistakable gift of oratory.

On 24 May 1921, Captain Gee's old division – 'the Incomparable 29th', which had been disbanded on 15 March 1919, was honoured by the people of Warwickshire. A monument, in Portland stone, was unveiled on the spot where King George V had reviewed his troops prior to the departure of the 29th Division for Gallipoli in March 1915. The

Captain and Mrs Gee at Burton Lazars, March 1921.
(LEICESTER MERCURY)

Above: The Palace of Westminster.
(DEREK SEATON)

monument represented a fitting and lasting tribute to one of the most illustrious units of the British Army to take part in the First World War.

The fighting record of the 29th Division proudly lives on as testimony to an elite infantry formation:

Gallipoli
13 Victoria Crosses were won including the famous "6 VCs before breakfast" which were awarded to officers and men of the 1st Battalion, Lancashire Fusiliers following their landing at W Beach, Cape Helles on 25 April 1915.

The Western Front
14 more Victoria Crosses were awarded which gave the 29th Division the proud distinction of having won more VCs than any other division during the Great War.

Casualties
The total casualties, throughout the war, was in the order of 94,000.

Captain Gee was back in Leicestershire again to participate in an important ceremony later that year. On Thursday, 24 November a huge gathering of people assembled at Countesthorpe to witness HRH the Duke of York (later King George VI) unveil the village War

Below: Monument to the 29th Division, near to Stretton-on-Dunsmore, Warwickshire. (DEREK SEATON)

Memorial at the conclusion of a busy itinerary, including a visit to the Cottage Homes. Upon arrival in the village square, the Duke was welcomed by Captain Gee who thanked him for his gracious presence and invited him to unveil the monument. The sombre moment was a highly significant one as people reflected that 187 men from the village had served their country, in the First World War and 47 of them had died in the cause of freedom. This was a very high proportion of deaths, of the total number of men who served, for a village the size of Countesthorpe. The Duke of York extended his sympathies to the relatives, who mourned the loss of their loved ones, and acknowledged his pride in the privilege, which the people of Countesthorpe had shown to him, in asking him to unveil the War Memorial in honour of the men who fell. He also declared he was: "Glad that so brave a gallant soldier (Captain Gee) should be their spokesman." (*Leicester Evening Mail* 24 November 1921)

The grey granite Maltese Cross was the work of the London based sculptor and contractor G Hale & Son, 365-367 Euston Road, NW1. The cost of the memorial amounted to £279-9s-10d which had been met by 284 public subscribers from the village.

Included among the names on the memorial was Private Norman Cyril John Harrison, the elder son of William and Sarah Harrison of the Cottage Homes. A plaque in memory of Norman Harrison had also been placed, by his parents, on the north wall inside St Andrew's Parish Church.

The following month Captain Gee was invited to unveil the War Memorial in the village of Swithland in Charnwood Forest, Leicestershire. Again, a large gathering of people witnessed the service. Captain Gee spoke of the sacrifices which had been made and said: "I would like to think that at least once a year the schoolchildren would be brought to the War Memorial and pay their respects to those who gave their lives for England's freedom." (*Leicester Mercury*, 5 December 1921) The

HRH the Duke of York (centre) at the unveiling of the Countesthorpe War Memorial, Captain Gee is on the extreme right of the picture.
(HENRIETTA SCHULTKA)

Left: The War Memorial, surrounded by wreaths, following the unveiling ceremony, Captain Gee is on the extreme left of the picture.
(HENRIETTA SCHULTKA)

Below: The Swithland War Memorial, Swithland, Leics.
(DEREK SEATON)

oak cross was positioned on the main street, next to the village hall, and stood on a pedestal with approaching steps of Swithland slate from the local quarry.

During May 1922 a branch of the British Legion was established in the House of Commons. The branch was specifically formed to provide membership for MPs and members of staff of the House. Field Marshal, Earl Haig attended at the invitation of Major Jack Ben Brunel Cohen, Member of Parliament for the Fairfield Division of Liverpool. Major Cohen served in the 5th Battalion King's (Liverpool Regiment), (Territorial Force), in Flanders where he lost both legs. He was elected to Parliament in December 1918. Captain Robert Gee was elected as the Honorary Treasurer of the new branch.

Captain Gee's commitments as the Member for East Woolwich continued to include his involvement in the controversial future of the Woolwich Arsenal. At the time of the Armistice, the whole of three gigantic factories had a capacity to employ 102,000 workers. By 1 April 1922 it was estimated that the workforce had dwindled to 12,000 operatives who continued to be concerned for their future.

The original Royal Arsenal Gatehouse, Beresford Square, Woolwich.
(DEREK SEATON)

The Countesthorpe Cottage Homes suffered a further grievous loss on 28 June when the Superintendent, William Harrison died. His death, whilst still in post, meant that his wife Sarah could no longer remain as Matron, since the posts continued to be joint-appointments, and she was obliged to leave the Cottage Homes.

On 6 October 1922, the Prime Minister David Lloyd George resigned following disapproval of his handling of the Chanak crises. The Conservative members of the Coalition Government had decided to withdraw their support for Lloyd George and he felt obliged to tender his resignation. He was succeeded by Andrew Bonar Law, the newly appointed leader of the Conservative Party, on 23 October. A General Election was called for 15 November and Captain Gee's opponent was Henry Snell. He was the son of an agricultural labourer and had begun work in the fields at the age of eight years. Henry Snell was another man who had risen from humble beginnings to carve out a successful career and had become a lecturer in economics to the Fabian Society. He had, unsuccessfully, contested Huddersfield in the General Elections held in January and December 1910 and in the 'Coupon Election' of 1918.

On this occasion the Labour Party's candidate for East Woolwich proved to be a more formidable opponent and, in keeping with Labour gains nationally, the constituency chose to give its support to Henry Snell. There was an 80% poll in East Woolwich and the count took place at the Town Hall. The result was announced, at 12.30 am, on 16 November:

Henry Snell (Labour)	15,620
Captain Robert Gee, VC, MC (Conservative)	<u>11,714</u>
Labour majority	3,906

The Coalition Government was finally rejected and many of those who had supported Lloyd George, including Captain Gee, were casualties in the 1922 General Election. Andrew Bonar Law led the Conservative Party to victory with 347 seats (an overall majority of 77) and was confirmed as Prime Minister. The Labour Party, who secured 142 seats, became the official opposition and included, once again, in their ranks, was Ramsay MacDonald after his victory at Aberavon where he had a majority of 3,207 votes over his Conservative opponent. Thus Captain Gee's tenure of office, as the Member of Parliament for East Woolwich, came to an abrupt end after only twenty months. During that time he had worked hard for the constituency and the Conservative Party fulfilling speaking engagements, of which he received a great number, all over the country.

He had scarcely had time to recover from losing his seat before he was back electioneering once again. A vacancy suddenly arose at East Newcastle-upon-Tyne following the death of the sitting member, Joseph Nicholas Bell who died on 17 December 1922. Joseph Bell had won the seat for the Labour Party, in the General Election, less than five weeks earlier. A by-election was called for 17 January 1923 and three candidates were adopted: Captain Robert Gee (Conservative), Arthur Henderson (Labour) and Major Harry Barnes (Liberal). Unemployment was the key issue in this Labour stronghold. Arthur Henderson was first elected to Parliament, for Barnard Castle, in 1903. He was the leader of the Labour Party from 1914 to 1917 and a member of the War Cabinet 1916-17. Along with Ramsay MacDonald, Henderson had lost his seat in the General Election of 1918 and had again been unsuccessful at Widnes in 1922. He was, nevertheless, another formidable political opponent.

Captain Gee was supported at a number of his meetings by Arthur Neville Chamberlain, the Conservative MP for the Ladywood Division of Birmingham, who was destined to be a future Prime Minister. On the day prior to the by-election Captain Gee received a letter from the Prime Minister, Andrew Bonar Law which was reported in *The Times* and contained heartfelt words of encouragement: "You are proving a frank and fearless exponent of Conservative and Unionist principles and you have my heartfelt good wishes for your success in the strenuous contest in which you are engaged."

The result in East Newcastle-upon-Tyne, once again, went against Captain Gee:

Arthur Henderson (Labour)	11,066
Major Harry Barnes (Liberal)	6,682
Captain Robert Gee, VC, MC (Conservative)	6,480
Labour majority:	4,384

In May 1923, Andrew Bonar Law was diagnosed as suffering from cancer of the throat, he resigned immediately and was succeeded, as Prime Minister, by Stanley Baldwin on 21 May. The former Prime Minister died on 30 October and was buried in Westminster Abbey.

After only seven months in office, Baldwin decided to go to the country to ask the electorate for support to introduce a policy of fiscal protection (tariffs) in order to combat unemployment more effectively. The date of the General Election was set for 6 December. On this occasion Captain Gee was adopted as the Conservative candidate for the Bishop Auckland Division of County Durham. His opponents were Benjamin Charles Spoor (Labour) and J. Bainbridge (Liberal).

Benjamin Spoor, who was born at nearby Witton Park in 1878, had won the seat from the sitting Liberal member in December 1918 and had successfully retained his seat in the 1922 General Election. For the third time Captain Gee had to concede defeat in the Labour heartland of the North-East in December 1923:

Benjamin Charles Spoor (Labour)	13,328
J. Bainbridge (Liberal)	6,686
Captain Robert Gee, VC. MC (Conservative)	6,024
Labour majority:	6,642

The General Election of December 1923 was inconclusive with no single party securing a majority. Baldwin's Conservative administration only lasted until 21 January 1924 when it was defeated in the House of Commons by 72 votes. Ironically, it was Robert Gee's old political opponent Ramsay MacDonald, who was summoned by the King and sworn in as the first Labour Prime Minister on 22 January 1924. There is no record of congratulations or commiserations being exchanged between the former candidates at East Woolwich!

1924 was to prove to be a far happier year for the gallant soldier endeavouring to establish himself as a professional politician. Two events occurred which were to bring him both personal happiness and the opportunity, once more, to enjoy the political limelight. On 7 June his elder daughter, Edith Tannycastell Gee married Douglas William Harrison at the Parish Church of All Saints, Twickenham. Edith was aged 21 years and her husband Douglas, an engineer, was 24 years of age. The marriage brought together the surviving son of the former senior officers of the Countesthorpe Cottage Homes and the daughter of one of the former boys, who had been admitted there as an 11 year old orphan 37 years earlier.

One notable guest at the wedding was Major Edward Beckwith who had served in the Royal Fusiliers with the bride's father. Major Beckwith had joined the regiment in 1894 and served in the ranks for 21 years and 149 days prior to being granted a commission, in the 2nd Battalion, on 21 May 1915 – the same day his friend WO II Robert Gee was commissioned. They served together at Gallipoli where the then Acting Captain Beckwith saved Captain Gee's life in the trenches. The incident occurred when Captain Gee was about to be stabbed by a Turkish soldier whereupon his fellow Fusilier shot and killed his friend's assailant. Captain Beckwith retained the Turkish dagger and decided to bring it along to the wedding where he duly offered it to the bride for her to cut her wedding cake with it. The dagger was accepted as a gift but the suggestion that it should be used as a replacement knife, to cut the wedding cake, was politely declined!

Captain Gee having fought, unsuccessfully, in two Labour Party strongholds during 1923 was then presented with the chance to mount a more serious challenge in a rural constituency back in his native county. In August 1924 he was selected to fight the Bosworth Division of Leicestershire on behalf of the Conservative Party. The constituency was held by the Liberal Party between the General Elections of 1906 and 1922 when the Conservative candidate won the seat. In the General Election of December 1923 Bosworth had been regained for the Liberal Party by George Ward, a local boot manufacturer from the village of Barwell situated within the constituency.

Having accepted the challenge, Captain Gee paid his first visit to the constituency on 12 August, when he declared, at Hinckley, that he was: "greatly honoured to have been selected as their standard-bearer in the coming fight." He outlined his policies in some detail and promised to mount an extensive tour of the area and gave an assurance that, if elected, he would be "a full-time politician."

All of this was the prelude to an imminent General Election. Ramsay MacDonald, who held both the office of Prime Minister and Foreign Secretary, carried a heavy burden of responsibility. On 8 October 1924 the minority Labour Government lost a Vote of Censure in the House of Commons by 344 votes to 198. The King, acting on the advice of the Prime Minister, dissolved Parliament on 9 October and another General Election was called, the date being fixed for Wednesday 29 October.

The Guardian and South Leicestershire Advertiser reported, on 10 October, that: "Captain Gee is the prospective Conservative candidate and has already become a familiar figure on Conservative platforms throughout the Division." Three days later a meeting was held of the Council of the Bosworth Division Conservative and Unionist Association at the Leicester Constitutional Club.

The meeting was presided over by Lieutenant-Colonel E.C. Atkins and the resolution, adopting Captain Robert Gee as the Unionist candidate, was carried unanimously. Appropriately, Robert Gee received his endorsement in his native city and members were reminded: "In 1921 he had defeated the present Prime Minister at East Woolwich." (*The Guardian and South Leicestershire Advertiser* 17 October 1924).

His opponents were George Ward, the sitting Liberal member and John Minto the Labour Party candidate. There was every indication that the campaign would develop into a keenly contested affair. John Minto was born in Kilmarnock, Scotland on 18 November 1887, he was the youngest of six children and, like Robert Gee, came from humble origins and was very much a self-made man. In the First World War he served with the Royal Engineers and reached the rank of Sergeant. He was elected as a councillor on the Leicester City Council in November 1922.

Leicester Constitutional Club, 1 Pocklington's Walk, Leicester.
(DEREK SEATON)

Captain Gee immediately set out upon a series of speaking engagements throughout the constituency and made his position clear on the question of further military action when he addressed a meeting at Stanton-under-Bardon on 26 September. Captain Gee's comments were reported fully in *The Guardian and South Leicestershire Advertiser* whose readers were informed: "According to a report, the present member (George Ward) seemed to think that the only person who did not want war was a Liberal. No man, whether a temporary soldier, a conscript or a regular like myself, wants another war. I have seen at least as much as most people of war, and you take it from me that the last thing I want to see is another war." He also declared his belief in the British Empire and articulated his views on the Capitalist system, unemployment, education and housing provision.

Captain Gee made a record tour of the constituency, by motor car on 23 October wearing a large blue horseshoe decorated with white heather sent from Covent Garden by a "porter pal admirer". On Tuesday evening 28 October, the eve of the General Election, Captain Gee accompanied by his daughter Amy toured the centre of Hinckley where both received injuries resulting from an accident which was featured in the *Hinckley Times and Bosworth Herald* (29 October 1924). The story was reported thus: "While nearing the close of his journey on Tuesday night, Captain Gee was temporarily knocked out through being thrown from the seat of his motor car owing to the bad state of the road. His head hit the roof of the car and he received a severe shock. He pluckily decided to continue his journey however, Miss Gee who was sitting by his side, was also thrown from her seat and sustained a blow on the head."

The Bosworth contest could not have developed into a more marginal affair and following, a cleanly-fought fight, Captain Robert Gee was the victor, on the day, by the slender majority

Councillor John Minto (He became an Alderman in 1944 and Lord Mayor of Leicester 1944-45).
(LEICESTER CITY COUNCIL)

of 358 votes in wresting the seat from George Ward who, in turn, polled a mere 613 votes more than Councillor John Minto. The result was published in the *Hinckley Times and Bosworth Herald* the following day and clearly showed the quite remarkable closeness between the three candidates:

HINCKLEY TIMES AND BOSW

Gee Wins Bosworth.
358 MAJORITY.

The Result of the Bosworth Division was declared at 7 p.m. last night as follows:

CAPT. ROBERT GEE (Cons.)	10,114
MR. GEORGE WARD (Liberal)	9,756
COUN. JOHN MINTO (Labour)	9,143
Conservative Majority over Liberal	358

CONSERVATIVE GAIN.

At the last Election on Dec. 6th, 1923, the result was—

MR. GEORGE WARD (Liberal)	11,596
MAJOR GUY PAGET (Conservative)	8,430
MR. E. HUGHES (Labour)	8,152
Liberal Majority	3,166

CAPT. R. GEE, M.P.

Above: Hinckley & District Constitutional Club, Station Road, Hinckley in the 1920s.
(HINCKLEY TIMES)

Right: A victorious Captain Robert Gee, MP for the Bosworth Division.
(LEICESTER MERCURY)

On the evening of the declaration Captain Gee set off on a celebratory tour of the constituency. Upon his arrival at the Hinckley Constitutional Club he told his followers: "It was indeed a proud fact that I have journeyed from Metcalf Street, Leicester to Westminster."

His tour of the constituency took him to Earl Shilton, Coalville and finally to Market Bosworth where he received "a splendid reception" from a huge crowd in the Market Place.

Captain Gee was back at Westminster for the second time having fought his sixth election campaign with the same tenacity as he frequently displayed when he was in action on the battlefields of Gallipoli and the Western Front. Undoubtedly, he would have reflected upon the fact that injuries could also occur in peacetime – certainly when electioneering at East Woolwich and Bosworth. It goes without saying that he would have made a note to speak to the Clerk of the Hinckley Urban District Council about the state of the roads in the town!

Another victor in the General Election of 19124 was Captain Gee's friend, William (later Sir William) Lindsay Everard who won the Melton Division of Leicestershire, for the Conservative Party with a majority of 5,156 votes over his Liberal opponent, Arthur Richardson. Lindsay Everard of Ratcliffe Hall, Leicestershire served, initially, as a Private with the Royal Fusiliers then the Leicestershire Yeomanry (Prince Albert's Own), where he rose to be the Adjutant, and finally the 1st Life Guards, during the First World War, and was a director of Everards Brewery Ltd, Leicester. Following their successes at Melton and Bosworth, Lindsay Everard gave Captain Gee a pair of cuff-links engraved with the words "To the victor of Bosworth from the victor of Melton Mowbray."

It is likely that Captain Gee, in addition to his friendship with Lindsay Everard, had connections with the Licensed Victuallers as he had been depicted in *Punch*, dated 28 June 1922, holding a foaming tankard of ale with the caption "Captain Gee, VC stands up for beer." Certainly, when old soldiers, from the Royal Fusiliers, called at the Captain's home in Twickenham to pay their respects all would be made welcome. Hospitality, accorded to former comrades, usually took the form of a glass of beer from barrels kept at the house and supplied by William Lindsay Everard.

Following his success at Bosworth Captain Gee was soon in evidence as he pursued his political mandate. During December 1924 he wrote letters to *The Times*, the correspondence was headed "Politics in Schools" and he set out his forthright views on the inequalities in the scales of teachers' salaries and gave his support to the concept of an annual exchange of teachers between Great Britain and the Dominions.

During 1925 Captain Robert Gee's achievements were recognised, in his home city of Leicester, when the Leicester City Council decided to confer upon him the Honorary Freedom of the City. At a meeting of the Council, at the Town Hall on 28 April 1925, the following resolution was moved by the Mayor, Councillor Herbert Simpson, seconded by Alderman Sir Jonathan North and carried:

> That this Council under and by virtue of the provisions of the Honorary Freedom of Boroughs Act 1885, in recognition of his eminent services to the Nation, do confer on Captain Robert Gee, Victoria Cross, Military Cross, Member of Parliament (Reserve of Officers), the Honorary Freedom of the City of Leicester, and do hereby accordingly admit him to be an Honorary Freeman of the City.
> (Leicester City Council, minute 227, 28 April 1925)

(The seconder of the motion, Alderman Sir Jonathan North was the wartime Mayor of Leicester who had accorded a Civic Reception for Captain Gee on 11 July 1918. Jonathan North was presented with the Honorary Freedom of the Borough of Leicester on 15 April 1919 and was Knighted by King George V, on 10 June 1919, in the De Montfort Hall, Leicester. Following the visit of the King to Leicester, the old County Borough was granted the status of City in July 1919).

A special meeting of the City Council was held at the Lecture Hall of the Museum Buildings in New Walk, on 22 July 1925, when the Honorary Freedom of the City was presented to Captain Gee and four other recipients: Thomas Fielding Johnson, MA, JP, Charles Bond, CMG, MRCS, The Reverend Canon James Went, MA, and the Reverend Canon Edward Atkins, BSc. Each received "the resolution conferring upon him the Honorary Freedom of the City with the casket for its retention." (Leicester City Council report, 22 July 1925) [See Appendix III]

In addressing the distinguished gathering the Mayor, Councillor Herbert Simpson referred to Captain Gee's humble beginnings, his placement in Leicester Workhouse and the Countesthorpe Cottage Homes followed by his outstanding military career and his greatest distinction – the award of the Victoria Cross. Having read the official report of the action, which led to the award, the Mayor said to Captain Gee: "We are proud to observe that you have been made a Life Member of the Naval & Military Club, an honour only conferred previously upon Princes of the Blood Royal, Field Marshals and Admirals." The Mayor concluded: "Captain Gee, we ask you to do us the honour to accept the Honorary Freedom of the City of Leicester, the greatest distinction we, your fellow-citizens, can bestow."

Captain Gee, in reply, expressed his gratitude for the great honour conferred upon: "One of Leicester's most humble sons." He went on to say: "In a gathering so representative as this, embracing as it does the Church, Commerce, Medicine, Education and the Forces of the Crown, I can only imagine that I am included in this select gathering because it was my good

The Lecture Hall, New Walk Museum, Leicester.
(DEREK SEATON)

fortune to obtain a decoration which, I earnestly assure you, thousands earned but few secured. And so, by honouring me, I perceive my native City is honouring all those who fought and suffered for our beloved Country."

On the casket, containing the scroll, which was presented to Captain Gee: "The Victoria Cross and the Military Cross were featured in enamel. Laurel wreaths further enriched the hand-wrought silver casket which was on a plinth of satin wood." (*Leicester Mercury*, 22 July 1925) Captain Gee was only the 14th person to receive the Honorary Freedom of the City of Leicester and only the third soldier to be honoured, following in the footsteps of Colonel John Edward Sarson (1903), and his Commander-in-Chief, Field Marshal Sir Douglas Haig (Earl Haig of Bemersyde) who received his Freedom on 7 April 1922.

The year 1925 also marked Captain Gee's discharge from the Reserve List of Officers. He was finally discharged on 8 May upon entering his fiftieth year thereby reaching the age limit for recall.

Late night sittings at the House of Commons, at which Captain Gee was in almost constant attendance, began to take their toll. He continued to suffer from the effects of his war wounds and, on one occasion during a lengthy sitting, he collapsed in the Chamber. Despite these difficulties he was always willing to assist other members of the Conservative Party as was instanced in the *Bury and Norwich Post*, dated 8 January 1926, which reported: "Captain Gee, VC, MC, MP, who has spoken several times at Bury St Edmunds and assisted Lieutenant-Colonel Guinness in his recent by-election campaign has been injured by a fall after a heart seizure at Leicester Station." Lieutenant-Colonel, the Right Honourable Walter Edward Guinness, DSO, had served in the Suffolk Yeomanry (The Duke of York's Own Loyal Suffolk Hussars) in the Boer war and the First World War in which he was awarded the DSO in 1917 and Bar in 1918. He was elected as a Conservative Member of Parliament for the Bury St Edmunds Division of Suffolk in August 1907 and, whilst he enjoyed a comfortable majority in his constituency, he was immensely grateful to Captain Gee for his valuable support.

By April of 1926 rumours had begun to circulate to the effect that Captain Gee was proposing to resign his seat in parliament. *The Times*, dated 21 April, declared: "there is no truth in the report circulated yesterday that Captain Gee, VC proposes to resign his seat in Parliament forthwith." The report went on to say, however, that he would be absent from his Parliamentary duties "for at least three months owing to ill-health." A further report in *The Morning Post*, of the same date, informed its readers that Captain Gee had authorised a denial of the report that he was thinking of resigning his seat at Bosworth adding: "that acting on medical advice, he is leaving for France tomorrow and will take a rest of about three months." The article described him as "a hard worker for the Conservative cause, ever since the war, and is most popular with his fellow-members."

Shortly afterwards Captain Gee applied for and was granted a year's leave of absence by the Government Whips. The decision was taken on health grounds whereupon Captain Gee left suddenly for Australia in order to have a prolonged holiday and rest. His departure came as a great shock to his family and Mrs Gee did not accompany him to Australia. Captain Gee's colleagues and constituents were also amazed by his decision, not least because of his regular attendances and contributions as a greatly respected Member of Parliament. Upon leaving England he resigned all of his Masonic memberships, the highlight of which had been in 1921 when he was rewarded by Grand Lodge by being appointed Assistant Grand Sword Bearer.

6
A NEW LEASE OF LIFE

Captain Gee sailed for Australia on the SS *Ormonde* bound for Perth, the capital of Western Australia. During the long sea voyage he was taken seriously ill and had to be taken off the ship, when it docked at Fremantle, and admitted direct to hospital for emergency medical treatment. He spent some time in Perth under the care of the physicians due to his poor physical condition. A period of medical attention was required for the treatment of the wounds he had sustained to his head and stomach, on the battlefields of France, to which he responded well and made a good recovery.

Captain Gee then began to turn his attention to earning a living in a new and strange environment. Having heard of an area of bush land due to be developed as individual farms at Mullewa, almost 300 miles north-east of Perth, he decided to take up the challenge of farming. He applied for, and was successful in obtaining, a 1600 acre block of virgin land on the Mendel's Estate at Mullewa, which had been purchased by the Australian Government. There together with a former Army friend, Sergeant Frederick Hills, who served with the Royal Fusiliers in France, he embarked upon one of the greatest challenges of his life. He had no knowledge of farming but, with his customary enthusiasm, he was stimulated by the sheer demands of the situation which would test him to the full.

On 13 September 1926 Captain Gee started to work on his holding in the bush. Initially, it meant living in a tent before a humble corrugated-iron shack, with only the earth to serve as a floor, could be erected to serve as a tiny farmhouse. He named his farm CAMBRAI perpetuating the French town and the battle where he was awarded his Victoria Cross.

Land had to be cleared, fences erected and water carted in order to prepare the holding for its first crop the following year. Robert Gee found the hot climate to his liking and conducive to his health to the extent that he began to think seriously about settling in Western Australia. Meanwhile, as he threw himself into his new lifestyle, with boundless enthusiasm, questions were being asked back in England regarding his future intentions, particularly in the Bosworth constituency where some of the electorate were becoming restless because they were no longer effectively represented in Parliament.

An article in the *Hinckley Times and Guardian*, dated 18 March 1927, ran the headline: "Where is Captain Gee?" Lieutenant-Colonel Atkins was asked "What would happen if Captain Gee did not return?" he replied that he could

A rejuvenated, smart-looking Captain Gee, wearing his medal ribbons, photographed with a young Australian worker at Geraldton, Western Australia on 25 April 1927.
(ROBERT HARRISON)

throw no light on the matter. As the President of the Bosworth Division Conservative and Unionist Association, Lieutenant-Colonel Atkins stated: "He had gone to Australia on a year's leave of absence. That year's life did not expire until May." He added that he was: "Inclined to think that after May Captain Gee would have resigned or come back."

By the spring of 1927 Captain Gee's health had improved considerably and he was looking and feeling fitter than at anytime since his ordeals at Gallipoli and on the Western Front.

Things finally came to a head on 10 May when it was announced in the *London Gazette* that the Chancellor of the Exchequer had appointed Captain Robert Gee, VC, MC, to be Steward and Bailiff of the Manor of Northstead. The *Hinckley Times and Guardian* picked up the announcement and explained to its readers: "this means that he has now tendered his resignation as the Conservative member (for Bosworth)." Captain Gee had, in effect, applied for the Chiltern Hundreds which enabled him to resign his seat as a Member of Parliament.

A writ for a by-election, to take place at Bosworth, was received by the deputy returning officer on 13 May, nominations were received on 23 May and Polling Day was fixed for 31 May. Another memorable fight took place in the Bosworth Division with the following result:

Sir William Edge (Liberal)	11,981
John Minto (Labour)	11,710
Brigadier-General Edward L. Spears (Conservative)	7,685
Liberal majority over Labour	271

Once again the Liberal Party had regained Bosworth having chosen to support Sir William Edge, who had previously sat in the House of Commons as MP for Bolton from 1916 to 1923.

Whilst Bosworth was changing its political allegiance, its former Member of Parliament was beginning to see the first fruits of his labours on his farm in far-distant Western Australia. A report in the *Melbourne Herald* (26 October 1927) gave an account of the progress he had made twelve months after he had commenced to clear and prepare his holding at Mullewa. The article described his enthusiasm and joy when he was able to "walk around a field of 100 acres of wheat growing chest high and fast taking the rich golden colour of fruition." The first hundred acres yielded a grain return of from 15 to 18 bushels to the acre cleared in 100 acre plots. His first year's endeavours, in the hot climate of Western Australia, had brought about a great improvement in his health and well-being and he described his feelings thus: "It is the first time in my life I have created anything."

However, despite all his hard work and the testing of his powers of endurance he was to become, like so many of his contemporaries, a victim of the worldwide economic crisis brought about by the Great Depression which started in the United States of America in October 1929. The effects of the Depression years were catastrophic upon the farming communities in Western Australia and wheat prices slumped to next to nothing. Captain Gee, along with countless other farming entrepreneurs, was forced to give up his holding and literally walked from his farm penniless in 1934. At 58 years of age with no financial resources and no other trade to fall back upon he faced a bleak future in a country where there was no form of Government Social Security at that time. Eventually he found board accommodation in a village near Perth before moving on to a small weatherboard cottage in the hills area some 20 miles east of Perth.

Another three years passed before he obtained work in the form of a temporary job, during the pre-Christmas shopping period, in the despatch department of Boans Limited, one of the largest department stores in Perth. The firm specialised in the sale of high quality games and leisure activity equipment which included darts and dartboards, indoor bowls, quoits and other games as well as target rifles and ammunition.

Sometime later when Frank Boan, the Managing Director of Boans Ltd heard that a holder of the Victoria Cross had been employed in a temporary capacity in the store, from time to time, he created a new post of Staff Welfare Officer which he offered to Captain Gee in 1940. He, in turn, gratefully accepted this unexpected, permanent position which offered him both security and yet another challenge.

After a lengthy silence during the Second World War, news of Captain Gee was received in Leicester, in March 1946, in the form of a letter which he wrote to the Lord Mayor, Councillor Charles Edward Worthington CBE, in which he described his work, in Australia during the war.

Councillor Worthington, also a native of Leicester, was another veteran who had distinguished himself in the First World War. He was commissioned into the Royal Flying Corps in 1916 and served as a fighter pilot in France and Belgium. He was officially credited with several air victories.

Captain Gee's letter, contained specific references to Leicestershire, and was published in the *Leicester Mercury* (5 March 1946). In his letter to the Lord Mayor he commented: "Of the many honours which fortune has favoured me with, the one I most value is having been made a Freeman of my native city, and as such I think the folk at Leicester might be interested in my war work.

"I put my age back ten years in order to join the Volunteer Defence Corps, but was rejected on medical grounds. I was then appointed Welfare Officer to Boans Limited, Perth, Western Australia. The average number of staff from January 1940 to January 1946 was 750."

He went on to say: "The executive of the firm have lavishly entertained the men of the Royal Navy, who have called into Fremantle, and amongst them have been a few from Leicester, Hinckley and Countesthorpe."

Captain Gee was a popular figure in Perth where he continued to pursue a wide range of interests which included involvement in the local political scene.

Captain Gee finally retired from his post with Boans Ltd in 1951, aged 75 years. He had served as the firm's first Welfare Officer for 11 years and during that time, he had gained the respect and admiration of the management and his colleagues as he carried out his duties with his usual willingness and efficiency.

He spent his retirement in his neat, tidy cottage named DUNMUVING in Orange Road, Darlington, a small town situated in the Darling Ranges

Left: Councillor Charles Edward Worthington, CBE, Lord Mayor of Leicester 1945-46.
(LEICESTER CITY COUNCIL)

Below: Captain Gee preparing to hand out literature in support of Gordon Hack, the Liberal Party candidate in Perth in 1948 (there was no Conservative Party in Australia).
(ROBERT HARRISON)

Captain Gee and a friend walking in Murray Street, Perth late 1940s.
(ROBERT HARRISON)

Captain Gee, aged 75 years, giving a speech at a wedding in Perth in December 1951.
(ROBERT HARRISON)

overlooking Perth. Being a good conversationalist and raconteur, Captain Gee always attracted an interesting and stimulating small group of friends who were received warmly into a homely, friendly atmosphere.

Although retirement was quietly enjoyed, Captain Gee remained active and his services continued to be in demand. He forged important links with the Australian Jewish Ex-servicemen's associations. In 1944 he had accepted the position of Vice President of the West Australian Council of Jewish Affairs and, in 1951, he was made a Life Member and Patron of the West Australian Jewish Ex-servicemen's Association.

In 1953 Captain Gee was appointed Commissioner for Declarations, Western Australia, a position which reflected the esteem in which he was held in his adopted country. He had a wide range of interests which included listening to every radio news bulletin. Not surprisingly, political broadcasts were his favourite and he was always poised to add his views, whether in agreement with the broadcasters or when he felt the urge to argue, vehemently, with opinions which conflicted with his own. He also enjoyed walking and had a passion for cricket. Above all he typified the spirit of those who fought, so magnificently, in the First World War and he retained his intense sense of loyalty to the Crown, the British Empire and his Regiment.

Anzac Day, held on 25 April each year (the anniversary of the Australian and New Zealand troops gallantry storming the beaches, on the first day of the landings, at Gallipoli in 1915) witnessed the annual military parades throughout the Australian cities. Captain Gee, together with Australian holders of the Victoria Cross, proudly led the parade in Perth. Even in his advanced years he continued to retain his military bearing at all times.

In 1956, Captain Gee was destined to take part in an unprecedented military occasion in London, where the Victoria Cross Centenary Review was to be held. When the Australian Government announced that all of the country's VC holders would be provided with free passage to England, for the Centenary celebrations, Captain Gee made application and was invited to travel with his Australian comrades. He declared that he had nothing but praise for the courtesies extended to him by the Australian Government and added: "Because I am a VC holder I am entitled to a free travel warrant anywhere in the country."

He joined twelve other winners of the Victoria Cross from the states of Western Australia and Victoria as this unique party assembled to make the long journey, by sea, on the RMS *Orcades* bound for England.

The *Orcades* docked at Tilbury on 4 June 1956. Captain Gee was duly met, at St Pancras station, by his grandson Robert N. Harrison. The occasion marked their first meeting for 30 years, for when Captain Gee left for Australia, in 1926, his grandson was little more than a year old. Upon arrival back in Leicester Captain Gee was reunited with his elder daughter, Edith Harrison and her husband, Douglas. He was much in demand by the local newspapers who descended upon the Harrison's home, at 20 Highgate Drive, Leicester both to interview and photograph the only Leicester born man ever to be awarded the Victoria Cross.

A *Leicester Mercury* reporter visited Captain Gee the following day and the evening edition of the newspaper gave an account of his life. The reporter described Captain Gee as "looking fit and suntanned", although he was still recovering from having had more shrapnel removed from his stomach wall, prior to leaving Western Australia, and was continuing to have the wound dressed each day. Commenting upon his sudden departure for Australia, thirty years earlier, he explained there was really no mystery involved. He also told the *Leicester Mercury* reporter: "I gained a new lease of life in Australia." Captain

The Western Australia and Victorian VC holders on RMS Orcades pictured with the ship's captain.
Back row (left to right): Private Richard Kelliher, VC, Lieutenant Clifford W.K. Sadlier, VC, Private Leslie T. Starcevich, VC, Private John Carroll, VC, Lieutenant George M. Ingram, VC, MM, Captain Smith of the Orcades, Private William Jackson, VC, Corporal George J. Howell, VC, MM, Lance-Corporal Thomas L. Axford, VC, MM.
Front row (left to right): Private Edward Kenna, VC, Private James P. Woods, VC, Captain Robert Gee, VC, MC, Lieutenant Rupert V. Moon, VC, Lieutenant William D. Joynt, VC.

(ROBERT HARRISON)

Captain Robert Gee photographed with his daughter, Edith Harrison, son-in-law Douglas Harrison and his grandson, Robert Harrison on 4 June 1956.
(LEICESTER MERCURY)

Gee later informed readers of the *Leicester Graphic* magazine (July 1956) that it was "fantastic" to suggest that he had disappeared as he had the Conservative Whips' permission to go to Australia on account of his health.

Captain Gee's return to his native city also enabled him to participate in a unique civic event. The Lord Mayor of Leicester, Alderman Alfred Halkyard having heard, on 4 June, that Captain Gee had arrived in the city that day immediately announced that he wished to bring together the three surviving holders of the Honorary Freedom of the City. On Tuesday 19 June the Lord Mayor received the Honorary Freemen at the Town Hall. The three distinguished guests of the Lord Mayor consisted of Harry Percy Gee (no relation to Robert Gee), Alderman Thomas Rowland Hill and Captain Robert Gee.

Harry Percy Gee, CBE, JP, was a Leicester born man (1874) who, upon completing his education, joined the family business of Stead & Simpson Ltd, boot and shoe manufacturers and retailers, with a chain of shops throughout the country, where he went on to become the Managing Director. He was a founder member of the Leicester and Rutland University College which opened in 1921 and he received his Honorary Freedom on 29 March 1950. Alderman Thomas Rowland Hill, CBE, JP, another Leicester born man (1885), held a number of important posts connected with the Building and Shopfitting Industry. He was elected to the City Council in 1926 and elevated to the Aldermanic Bench in November 1945. Alderman Hill was Lord Mayor of Leicester in 1951 and was presented with the Honorary Freedom of the City on 14 May 1956, just a month earlier than the unique gathering which took place on 19 June 1956.

The Lord Mayor, Alderman Alfred Halkyard also had a distinguished military career. He was commissioned into the 4th Battalion, the Leicestershire Regiment in 1916. He served in France and Belgium with the 8th Battalion from October 1916 to May 1918 when he was taken prisoner of war. Alderman Halkyard was awarded the Military Cross in May 1918.

The informal gathering brought together four eminent men, all of whom were born in Leicester, who had each achieved great things in their respective careers. By 1956 twenty-four men had received the Honorary Freedom of the City. It would not have escaped Captain Gee's notice that his old political adversary, the late James Ramsay MacDonald had also received the Honorary Freedom of the City on 6 November 1929 having, by that time, become Prime Minister for the second time.

Two days later, on 21 June, Captain Gee attended a reception, given in his honour, at the Leicester Synagogue by the Leicester branch of the Association of Jewish Ex-servicemen. The chairman, Bernard Barnett informed the assembled gathering that Captain Gee had accepted the honorary office of Life Vice-President of the Leicester branch of the Association. In reply, Captain Gee expressed his appreciation of the warm welcome he had been given by the Jewish community after so many years away from the City.

The three surviving holders of the Honorary Freedom of the City with the Lord Mayor of Leicester, at the Town hall, on 19 June 1956. (left to right) Alderman Thomas Rowland Hill, CBE, JP, Harry Percy Gee, CBE, JP, Captain Robert Gee, VC, MC, and the Lord Mayor, Alderman Alfred Halkyard, CB, MC, TD, DL, LL.B.
(LEICESTER MERCURY)

Captain Gee had served with many soldiers from the Jewish community, some of whom left their homes in the East End of London to join the ranks of their local Regiment, the Royal Fusiliers. During the First World War the Royal Fusiliers had, within their formations, 5 battalions which were comprised of men from the Jewish community, the 38th (Jewish), 39th (Jewish), 40th (Jewish), 41st (Jewish) Training Reserve and the 42nd (Jewish) Training Reserve.

Having received accolades from those in his native city, for which he was extremely grateful, Captain Gee returned to London for the great gathering of the holders of the Victoria Cross. His arrival in the metropolis also enabled him to be re-united with his younger daughter, Mrs Amy Andrews. Amy had trained as a nurse at St George's Hospital, London and later went into private nursing. She married her husband, Francis Joseph Andrews, in 1936. Captain Gee remained quite independent and stayed at the Regent Palace Hotel, in Oxford Street, whilst using London as a base for visiting old friends.

The VC Centenary celebrations covered a three day period from Tuesday 25 to Thursday 27 June. Initially a Service of Thanksgiving, to commemorate the Centenary of the Institution of the Victoria Cross, was held in Westminster Abbey on 25 June. Some 300 holders of the VC together with 900 relatives of the living, those deceased and the posthumous winners of the decoration were present in the huge congregation which included Ministers of State, Service Chiefs and the Lord Mayor of London. The address was

Below: The Leicester Synagogue, Highfield Street, Leicester. (Arthur Wakerley 1898).
(DEREK SEATON)

The Queen inspecting the holders of the Victoria Cross, drawn up on Hyde Park, accompanied by Lieutenant-General Lord Freyburg. Captain Gee is standing in the rear rank, wearing a bowler hat and behind the Gurkha soldier. 26 June 1956
(© THE TIMES/ LONDON)

given by the Archbishop of Canterbury, the Most Reverend Dr Geoffrey Francis Fisher.

Following the Service of Thanksgiving, the elite gathering of gallant men proceeded to the House of Commons where a Government Reception awaited them. There they were greeted by Sir Walter Monckton, Minister of Defence, on behalf of the Royal Society of St George. The principal hosts were the Prime Minister, the Right Honourable Sir Anthony Eden and Lady Eden. The opportunity to meet and chat with holders of the Victoria Cross was an occasion of great joy for both Sir Anthony Eden and Sir Walter Monckton. Each of them had distinguished war records, the Prime Minister was commissioned into the 21st (Service) Battalion (Yeoman Rifles) of the King's Royal Rifle Corps in 1915 whilst Sir Walter Monckton gained a commission in the Queen's Own (Royal West Kent Regiment) during 1914. Both were awarded the Military Cross on the Western Front and, by 1918, Anthony Eden had become the youngest Brigade-Major in the British Army.

The following day witnessed the highlight of the celebrations when the 300 holders of the Victoria Cross assembled for the great review, which was held in the presence of Queen Elizabeth II in Hyde Park. Appropriately, the weather on Wednesday 26 June was perfect as thousands of people gathered to witness the parade to mark the Centenary of the Institution of the Victoria Cross, and to see the proud holders, from all over the world, form up in order to be honoured by their Sovereign. Each of the three fighting services provided a Guard of Honour which consisted of 3 officers and 100 rank and file with band and colour. The Guard of Honour stood, with arms presented, as the VC holders marched on to parade led by the band of the Royal Marines playing "Sons of the Brave."

The parade was inspected by the Queen accompanied by the Duke of Edinburgh and Lieutenant-General Lord Freyberg, VC, DSO and 3 Bars.

Marlborough House, Pall Mall, London SW1.
(DEREK SEATON)

Also present on the royal dais were Queen Elizabeth The Queen Mother, Princess Margaret, the Duke and Duchess of Gloucester, the Princess Royal and the Duchess of Kent. They were accompanied by the Prime Minister, Sir Anthony Eden with several of the Prime Ministers from the Commonwealth, who were in London for the Commonwealth Prime Ministers' Conference, and Sir Winston Churchill.

The Queen having inspected the parade, paid tribute to the 1,344 men who had been awarded the Victoria Cross during the first 100 years since its inception, by Royal Warrant, on 29 January 1856. In referring to all recipients, over the century, the Queen said: "Their stories are linked by a golden thread of extraordinary courage." The parade was concluded by a grand march past at which the Queen took the salute.

Following the parade the VC holders and their relatives were entertained by the Government at a garden party and tea, given in their honour, at Marlborough House. The event was attended by Queen

The Guildhall, Gresham Street, London EC2.
(DEREK SEATON)

Elizabeth The Queen Mother, The Princess Royal and the Duke and Duchess of Gloucester.

The Victoria Cross Centenary Exhibition, staged in Marlborough House, was viewed by the guests and then remained open to the public until the end of July.

The Centenary celebrations were concluded with two events on Thursday 27 June. The VCs and their relatives were taken by train to Windsor Castle where they visited the state apartments and were entertained to tea in St George's Hall. To conclude three eventful and unparalleled days, the holders of the Victoria Cross and their wives were the guests at an Evening Reception given by the Lord Mayor of London at the Guildhall. The glittering occasion was attended by the Lord and Lady Mayoress, the Sheriffs and their ladies, Ambassadors, High Commissioners and high-ranking officers of the Armed Forces. The orchestra of the Royal Regiment of Artillery played during the evening.

During the remainder of his time in London, Captain Gee took the opportunity to visit old friends and to renew acquaintances with former comrades with whom he had served. His arrival back in England had not escaped the notice of many veterans from his old regiment and those of other regiments who had fought alongside the 2nd Battalion, Royal Fusiliers. Many wished to see him or contact him before he returned to Australia.

A letter was published in the *Harrow Observer & Gazette*, on 14 June 1956, from former Private (6306) Jesse T. Cattermole of Wealdstone who had served with the 1/7th Battalion (T.F.), The Duke of Cambridge's Own (The Middlesex Regiment) in France. Private Cattermole related how Captain Gee won his Victoria Cross and went on to say: "I had the honour to cover him with Lewis gun fire when he won the award." He wrote to Captain Gee to wish him a happy stay back in England and received a letter of thanks from his daughter, Mrs Edith Harrison, in Leicester, to say that Captain Gee remembered his old comrade from the action at Masnieres. Private Cattermole concluded his letter by describing Captain Gee as: "One of the bravest men I have known."

One occasion which, undoubtedly, gave Captain Gee a great deal of pleasure was a brief but joyous reunion with Private Herbert (Harry) Niblett, his former batman, whom he visited at his home in Eltham, south-east London. Private Niblett served with the 23rd (Service) Battalion (1st Sportsman's), Royal Fusiliers and was with Captain Gee on the Western Front.

Captain Gee never lost his affection for his old regiment and paid a visit to the Regimental Headquarters of the Royal Fusiliers, at the Tower of London, during his stay in the capital. He was presented with a copy of Northcote Parkinson's book *"Always a Fusilier."*

Two World War One veterans reunited. On the left is Private Herbert Niblett with Captain Robert Gee, VC, MC, on the right.
(ROBERT HARRISON)

Royal Fusiliers Museum, HM Tower of London. (Built as the Officers' Mess in the mid 19th century) One of the four museums of the Royal Regiment of Fusiliers.
(DEREK SEATON)

He finally left England, for the last time, when he sailed for Australia on 17 July. Captain Gee's departure, with the returning Australian VC holders, was reported in the *Leicester Mercury* the following day. The article included a message from the City's VC hero and Honorary Freeman: "Through his daughter, Mrs Douglas Harrison, he has sent a thank-you message to the many people in Leicester, including the Lord Mayor, who had welcomed him during his stay."

Captain Gee's remaining years were spent quietly in his home in Darlington where he indulged himself in his great pastime, reading. A life-long interest in the written word had played no small part in equipping him to cope, more than adequately, with his military and political challenges and he had acquired an enormous amount of knowledge in the process. Seated in his favourite chair, smoking his beloved pipe, Captain Gee surrounded himself with his many reference books which he referred to with great regularity. Poetry, in particular, meant a great deal to him and his memory of verse was quite prodigious.

By the late 1950s his health had begun to decline and, on 30 January 1960, he was admitted to the Home of Peace, a residential home for elderly people situated in Thomas Street, Subiaco, a seaside suburb of West Perth.

Meanwhile, Captain Gee's daughter Mrs Edith Harrison had written to one of her father's friends in Western Australia to enquire what he might like for his 84th birthday. The reply was to the effect that his dearest wish would be for his daughter to hand-over his group of Army medals to his old regiment, the Royal Fusiliers. In accordance with Captain Gee's wishes, his daughter and grandson duly presented his medals to Colonel C.A.L. Shipley, DSO, the Regimental Secretary at the City of London Headquarters of the Royal Fusiliers at HM Tower of London in May 1960.

Captain Gee's set of medals:

Victoria Cross, Military Cross, 1914-15 Star, British War Medal, Victory Medal, Long Service & Good Conduct Medal, King Edward VII, King George VI and Queen Elizabeth II Coronation Medals.

The medals are now on display in the Regimental Museum and serve to remind visitors that Captain Gee was one of twenty recipients of the Victoria Cross won by the Royal Fusiliers (City of London Regiment) throughout their glorious history.

Other artefacts of Captain Gee have, subsequently, been handed over, by his family, to the Regimental Museum including the casket and scroll declaring his conferment of the Honorary Freedom of the City of Leicester, also the sabre which originally belonged to Lieutenant-Colonel Septimus Legge and the legendary Turkish dagger.

Captain Gee continued to be cared for by the staff of the Home of Peace as his health declined. The matron of the home knew him through his work, in Perth, as part of the war effort, during the Second World War. Six months after his admission to the Home of Peace, Captain Gee died, peacefully, at the home on 2 August 1960 aged 84 years.

Obituaries appeared in *The Times* and *The Daily Telegraph*, the following day, along with reports of his death and tributes in the *Leicester Evening Mail* and the *Leicester Mercury*. Tributes were also paid to his memory in the Australian newspapers. One death notice in the *West Australian* came from the West Australian Jewish ex-servicemen's Association and read: "A tribute to the memory of our esteemed Life Member, Captain Robert Gee, VC, MC."

The funeral service took place at the Crematorium Chapel, Karrakatta, Perth on 4 August. The service was conducted by the Anglican Archbishop of Perth, the Most Reverend Robert William Haines Moline, MC. The Archbishop, a native of Sudbury, Suffolk, served in the Rifle Brigade (The Prince Consort's Own), and was a fellow-holder of the Military Cross. He was granted the rank of Major on demobilisation having served in the Army from 1914 to 1919. Also in attendance, and marking a rare break with tradition, was Rabbi Rubin Zacks who spoke a few words of tribute in recognition of Captain Gee's steadfast friendship and regard for his Jewish comrades in arms. Following cremation, his ashes were scattered in the rose garden at the crematorium.

The following year a fitting tribute to Captain Gee, in the form of a Fountain of Memory, was unveiled in the grounds of the new R.S.L. (Returned Servicemen's League) War Veterans' Home at Mount Lawley, Perth, Western Australia. The fountain was financed by the staff and executive members of Boans Ltd and the dedication ceremony was held on Saturday, 11 March 1961. Bishop C.L. Riley dedicated the memorial fountain, following the official opening of the R.S.L. Veterans' Home, and said of Captain Gee: "There can be no finer tribute to a man who did his best for his fellows in war and peace than this, a fountain that keeps on running for a very fine gentleman and citizen."

The inscription on the fountain read:

The Fountain of Memory was erected by the Staff and Executive of Boans Limited, in proud and honoured memory of Captain Gee, VC, MC, who became the firm's first Welfare Officer (1940-51). He

The Fountain of Memory.
Standing behind the fountain are the Honourable Ray O'Connor, Minister for Transport, Major-General Sir Douglas Kendrew, Governor of Western Australia and Percy Preston, State President, The Returned Sailors', Soldiers' and Airmen's Imperial League of Australia.
(COURTESY WEST AUSTRALIAN NEWSPAPERS)

died on 2 August 1960, at the age of 84 years. Renowned for his courage and tenacity of purpose.

(Major-General Sir Douglas Kendrew, KCMG, CB, CBE, DSO, a former Tiger, went on to become the Colonel of the Royal Leicestershire Regiment 1963-65).

The fountain was designed to send water cascading from two ponds into a large ornamental lake in the peaceful gardens of the home. Unfortunately, after some years, considerable damage was caused to the fountain due to the bore water used in the project. Eventually, the fountain had to be removed and no longer exists. The plaque, which was originally located in the base of the fountain, has been placed in a Rotunda situated in the centre of a beautiful garden at the War Veterans' Home.

Possibly the finest tribute to Captain Gee, VC, MC, was, appropriately, contained in the words of his obituary, published in the *Royal Fusiliers Chronicle*, in 1960, the final paragraph of which read:

"He was in every way a most remarkable man, whose lack of education as a child only served to emphasise his natural strength of character, shrewdness and unremitting zeal. A man of whom his Regiment is justly proud."

Captain Robert Gee, VC, MC.
(THE ROYAL FUSILIERS MUSEUM)

APPENDIX I

THE BATTLEFIELD AREAS OF THE WESTERN FRONT

APPENDIX II
THE GALLIPOLI CAMPAIGN

APPENDIX III
ROLL OF HONORARY FREEMEN

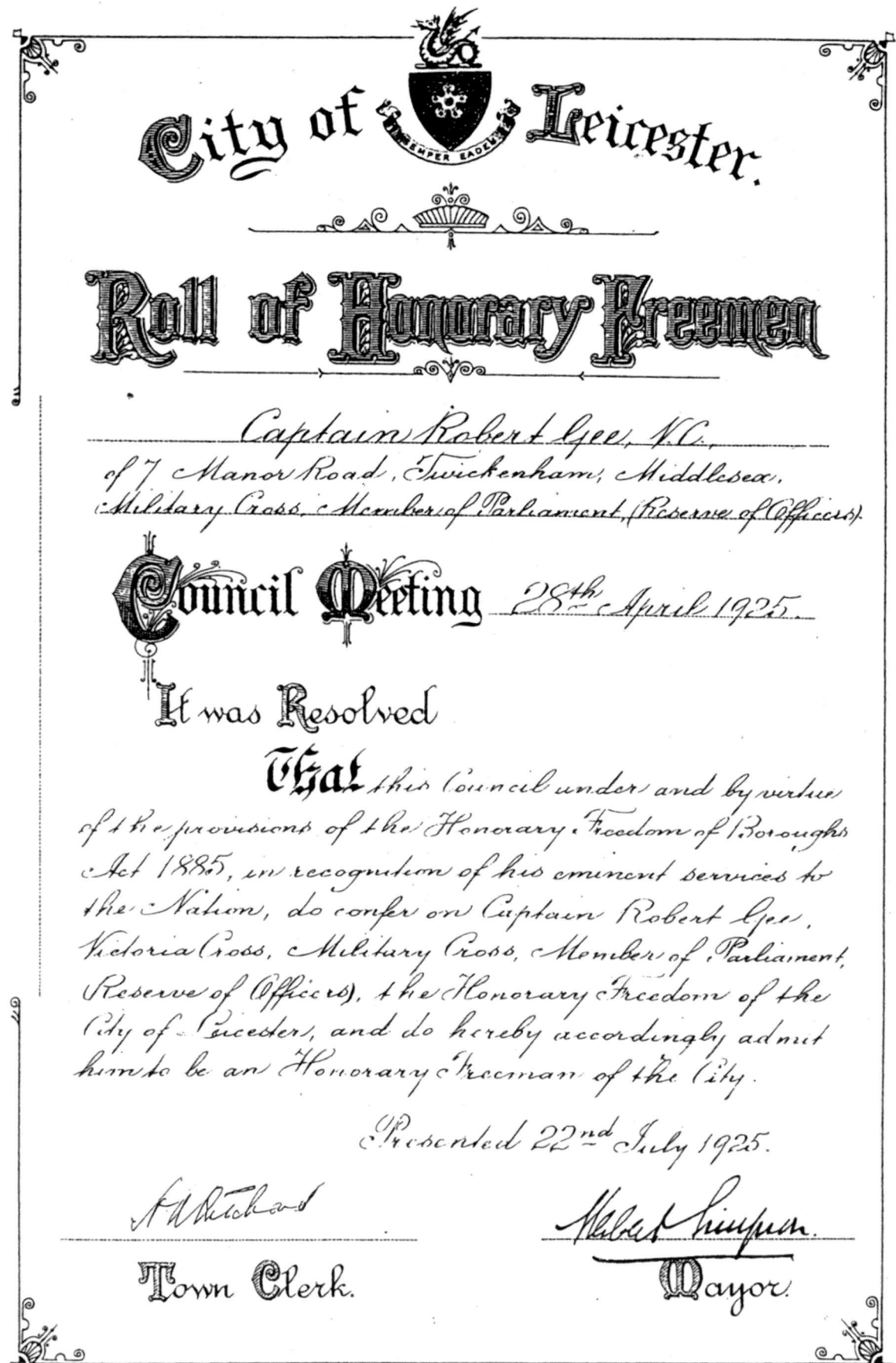

BIBLIOGRAPHY

Armitage, Francis Paul: *Leicester 1914-1918 : The Wartime Story of a Midland Town*. Leicester 1933

Beazely, Ben: *Four Years Remembered – Leicester During The Great War*. Derby 1999

Creagh, General Sir Garrett O'Moore & Humphris, E.M.: *The Victoria Cross and Distinguished Service Order*. London 1924

Foss, Michael: *The Royal Fusiliers*. London 1967

Gillon, Captain Stair: *The Story of the 29th Division*. London 1925

Holmes, Richard: *The Western Front*. London 1999

James, Brigadier E.A. *British Regiments 1914-1918 (5th Edition)*. Heathfield, East Sussex 1998

Marquand, David: *Ramsay MacDonald*. London 1977

O'Neill, H.C.: *The Royal Fusiliers in The Great War*. London 1922

Pevsner, Nikolaus, second edition revised by Williamson, Elizabeth: *The Buildings of Leicestershire and Rutland*. London 1992

Richardson, Matthew: *The Tigers*. Barnsley 2000

Saunders, Karen, Ambrose, Georgina and Payter, Charlotte: *The Countesthorpe Cottage Homes – A World Apart*. Countesthorpe 1996

Spurling, Major-General John Michael Kane: *The Tigers*. Leicester 1969

Webb, Lieutenant-Colonel Edward Arthur Howard: *History of the Services of the 17th Leicestershire Regiment 1688-1910*. London 1911

Wylly, Colonel Harold Carmichael: *History of the 1st and 2nd Battalions, The Leicestershire Regiment in The Great War*. Aldershot 1928

INDEX

Anderson, Lt-Gen Charles A.: 9
Andrews, Mrs Amy Tannycastell (née Gee): 67
Andrews, Francis Joseph: 67
Anstey, Leics: 30
Anzac Day: 64
Armitage, Francis Paul: 25
Atkins, Lt-Col E.C.: 56, 61, 62
Austin, Robert: 32
Australia: 61-66, 71-73
Australian Government: 61, 64, 65
Australian VC holders: 64, 65

Baldwin, Stanley: 55
Barradale, Isaac: 5
Bayfield, Lieut: 18. 19
Beaumont Hamel: 37
Beckwith, Major Edward: 55
Bedford Board of Guardians: 2, 3, 4
Bedford Union Workhouse: 2, 3, 4
Bell, Joseph Nicholas: 54
Bennett, Annie Susan (later Mrs William Billington & Mrs Thomas Buckingham): 2
Bennett family: 3
Billington, Annie Susan (née Bennett): 2, 3, 4
Billington, CSM Frank: 43, 44
Billington, Frederick Ernest (later Buckingham): 2, 3, 4
Billington, William Henry (later Buckingham): 2, 3, 4
Billington, William John: 2
Blackader, Lt-Col Charles Guinand (later Brig-Gen): 9, 15
Boan, Frank: 62
Boans Ltd, Perth: 62, 63, 72, 73
Bottomley, Horatio: 49
British Army:
    1st Army: 9, 10
    3rd Army: 38
    4th Army: 22, 24
    III Corps: 38, 39, 40
    IV Corps: 9, 10
    XIV Corps: 22
    Guards Division: 22
    6th Division: 22, 23, 24
    29th Division: 34, 37, 39, 50, 51
    71st Brigade: 22
    86th Brigade: 37, 38, 39
    87th Brigade: 38
    Dragoon Guards (King's)
        1st Bn: 40
    Dragoon Guards (Carabiniers)
        6th Bn: 32. 40

Duke of Cambridge's Own (The Middlesex Regt)
    1/7th Bn (TF): 70
    16th Bn: 38
Grenadier Guards
    1st Bn: 15
Guernsey Light Infantry: 38, 39
Hussars (Queen's Own)
    4th Bn: 32
King's (Liverpool Regt)
    1/5th Bn (TF): 53
King's Royal Rifles: 68
Lancashire Fusiliers
    1st Bn: 38, 51
Leicestershire Regiment
    1st Bn: 8, 21, 22, 23, 24, 25
    2nd Bn: 1, 7-10, 12, 14, 28, 43
    4th Bn: 66
    8th (Service) Bn: 66
Leicestershire Yeomanry (Prince Albert's Own): 58
Life Guards
    1st Bn: 58
London Rifles, The
    3rd Bn (TF): 10
Manchester Regiment: 42
Norfolk Regiment
    9th (Service) Bn: 22, 23
Queen's Own (Royal West Kent Regt): 45, 68
Rifle Brigade (The Prince Consort's Own): 72
Royal Fusiliers (City of London Regt)
    1st Bn: 33
    2nd Bn: 29, 32, 34-38, 70, 79
    4th Bn: 33
    6th Bn: 33
    6th Reserve Bn: 33
    23rd (Service) Bn (1st Sportsman's): 70
Jewish Bns
    38th, 39th, 40th, 41st, 42nd: 67
Royal Warwicks Regt
    1/6th Bn (TF): 44
Sherwood Foresters (Notts & Derbys Regt)
    2nd Bn: 22
South Wales Borderers: 35, 46
Suffolk Regiment
    9th (Service) Bn: 22
Suffolk Yeomanry (The Duke of York's): 60
Worcestershire Regiment
    3rd Bn: 9
British Expeditionary Force (BEF): 9

Buckingham, Ann: 3
Buckingham, Annie Susan (formerly Billington): 3,4,6,27
Buckingham, Frederick Ernest (formerly Billington): 4, 5, 6, 8
Buckingham, Jacob: 3
Buckingham, Joseph Henry: 4,6
Buckingham, Thomas Henry: 3, 4
Buckingham VC Memorial Fund: 26, 28
Buckingham, Private William Henry (formerly Billington)
    birth and early life – Bedford: 2-3
    move to Leicester: 4
    Countesthorpe Cottage Homes: 5-7
    enlisted into the Leics Regt: 7-8
    service 1901 to 1914: 8-9
    The Western Front: 9
    Neuve Chapelle: 9-11
    treatment for wounds: 12
    award of VC: 12
    receptions/presentations: 13-18
    recruitment duties: 18-21
    return to France: 21-22
    Battle of the Somme: 22-24
    death: 24
    tributes and memorials: 25-28
Byng, Lt-Gen (later Gen) Sir Julian: 36, 38

Cambrai: 38, 61
Carver, Walter: 41
Cattermole, Private Jesse T.: 70
Chamberlain, Arthur Neville: 54, 55
Cheape, Brigadier-Gen George, R.H.: 37, 38, 40
Chudleigh, Capt Cuthbert A.E.: 15
Churches:
    All Saints, Twickenham: 55
    Holy Trinity, Leicester: 3, 4
    St Andrew, Countesthorpe, Leics: 7, 27, 52
    St Botolph, Ratcliffe-on-the-Wreake, Leics: 49
    St Cuthbert, Bedford: 2
    St John, Bedford: 2
    St Mary, Anstey, Leics: 30
    St Thomas, South Wigston, Leics: 22
    Salem Baptist Chapel, Folkestone: 33
Churchill, Sir Winston Spencer: 69
Cohen, Major Jack B.B.: 53
Coleorton Hall, Leics: 18, 19
Connaught, Arthur Prince and Princess of: 46

Connaught, Duke of: 46
Countesthorpe Cottage Homes: 5-8, 12-14, 16, 17, 20, 24, 26, 27, 31, 32, 41-43, 51, 52, 54, 59
Countesthorpe village: 5, 7, 16, 27, 51, 63
Crooks, William: 17, 41, 48

Daily Mail: 13, 15
Daily Telegraph, The: 72
Dardenelles Expeditionary Force: 34
de Lisle, Maj-Gen Sir Beauvoir: 40
Distinguished Conduct Medal: 20, 21, 44
Dixon, Peter: 33
Dover, Kent: 33, 34, 37

Eden, Sir Anthony: 68, 69
Edge, Sir William: 62
Edinburgh, Prince Philip, Duke of: 68
Egypt: 8, 9, 34, 37
Elizabeth II: 68, 69
Elverdinghe: 37
Everards Brewery Ltd, Leicester: 58, 59
Everard, William (later Sir William) Lindsay: 49, 58, 59
Evershed, Arthur S. and Sarah: 32
Evershed, Sydney (alias): 32

Field Ambulances
   37th: 40
   88th; 37
   89th: 40
Fisher, Most Rev Dr Geoffrey Francis: 68
Flint, William: 4
Foulds, John: 30
Freemasons: 33, 37, 45, 60
French, Field-Marshal Sir John: 9
Freyberg, Col (later Lt-Gen Lord) Bernard, Cyril: 48, 68
Fuller, L/Cpl Wilfred Dolby: 15, 16

Gallipoli: 34-37, 50, 51, 55, 58, 61
Geary, Fred: 32
Gee, Amy (née Foulds): 30, 31
Gee, Amy Tannycastell (later Mrs Francis Andrews): 33, 40, 57
Gee, Edith Tannycastell (later Mrs Douglas Harrison): 33, 41, 42, 55
Gee, Elizabeth (née Dixon): 33, 41, 42, 50, 60
Gee, Elizabeth (Betsy) (later Mrs E. Linney): 31
Gee, Harry Percy: 66
Gee, Captain Robert
   birth: 30
   early life and family: 30-31
      Countesthorpe Cottage Homes: 31-32

   apprenticeships: 32
   enlisted 4th (Queen's Own) Hussars. 32
   enlisted Royal Fusiliers: 32
   service 1893 to 1914: 32-33
   marriage and family: 33
   Freemason: 33
   First World War: 33
   Gallipoli: 34-37
   Western Front: 37
   Beaumont Hamel: 37
   Military Cross: 37
   ADC to Prince of Wales: 37
   Cambrai: 38-40
   award of VC: 39-40
   admitted to Gray's Inn: 44
   receptions/presentations: 41-44, 46-47
   discharge from active service: 46
   Parliamentary Election campaigns:
      Consett Div of Durham 1918: 45
      East Woolwich 1921: 48-50
      East Woolwich 1922: 54
      East Newcastle-Upon-Tyne 1923: 54-55
      Bishop Auckland Div of Durham 1923: 55
      Bosworth Div of Leics 1924: 56-58
   MP for East Woolwich: 51-54
   MP for Bosworth: 57-62
   Honorary Freedom of the City of Leicester: 59-60
   move to Australia: 61
   life in Western Australia: 61-64
   VC Centenary Review, London 1956: 64-65
   visit to Leicester: 65-67
   Centenary celebrations: 67-71
   final years in Australia: 71-72
   death: 72
   tributes and memorial: 72-73
Gee, Robert snr: 33, 44
George V: 12, 15-17, 34, 40, 46-48, 50, 55, 56, 59
George VI: 28
German Army formations: 10, 24
Gillespie, Lt-Col Reginald H.: 24
Gillon, Captain Stair: 38
Glen Parva Barracks, Leics: 7, 12, 14, 18, 20-22
Gloucester, Duke and Duchess of: 69, 70
Gordon, Lt-Col Herbert: 15
Gray's Inn: 44, 45
Guardian & South Leics Advertiser, The: 56, 57
Guinness, Lt-Col Walter Edward: 60

Haig, Gen (later Field-Marshal) Sir Douglas: 9, 10, 38, 53, 60
Halkyard, Ald Alfred: 66, 71
Hamilton, Gen Sir Ian: 34
Harrison, Douglas William: 42, 55, 65
Harrison, Mrs Edith Tannycastell (née Gee): 55, 65, 70, 71
Harrison, Private Norman C.J.: 42, 52
Harrison, Robert N.: 65
Harrison, Sarah Jane: 7, 12-14, 16-18, 42, 52, 54
Harrison, William: 7, 9, 12-14, 16-18, 24, 42, 44, 52, 54
Hathern, Leics: 30
Henderson, Arthur: 54, 55
Henry, Prince (later Duke of Gloucester): 46
Herrick, Mrs: 43, 44
Hill, Ald Thomas Rowland: 66
Hills, Sgt Frederick: 61
Hinckley Echo: 20
Hinckley, Leics: 20, 57, 58, 63
Hinckley Times & Guardian: 61
Hinckley Times & Bosworth Herald: 57
House of Commons: 50, 53, 55, 58, 60, 62, 68
Hounslow Regimental Depot: 32, 33

Indian Army:
   Indian Army Corps: 9, 10
   7th Meerut Division: 9
   Bareilly Brigade: 9
   Dehra Brigade: 9
   Garhwal Brigade: 9
   39th Garhwal Rifles:
      1st Bn: 10
      2nd Bn: 10
   3rd Gurkha Rifles:
      2nd Bn: 10
   4th Gurkha Rifles:
      1st Bn: 10

Jewish Ex-servicemen: 64, 66, 67, 72
Jones, John: 33

Kendrew, Maj-Gen Sir Douglas: 73
Kent, Duchess of: 69
Kinton, Cllr George: 20, 21

Lane, Private Michael: 10, 19, 20
Lang, Bishop Norman: 27
Law, Andrew Bonar: 54, 55
Leicester Board of Guardians: 5, 6, 14, 17, 24, 26, 31, 32, 41
Leicester Chronicle: 4
Leicester City Council: 27, 28, 56, 59, 66, 72
Leicester Daily Mercury (later *Leicester Mercury*): 14, 17, 26, 42, 49, 52, 60, 63, 65, 71, 72

Leicester Daily Post: 10, 44
Leicester Evening Mail: 24, 43, 52, 72
Leicester Graphic: 66
Leicester Town Hall: 4, 41, 42
Leicester Union Workhouse: 4-6, 31, 32, 43, 59
Legge, Col George (Lord Dartmouth): 29
Legge, Major (later Lt-Col) Septimus Frederick: 40, 72
Les Rues Vertes: 38-40
Linney, Mrs Elizabeth (Betsy) (née Gee): 31
Lloyd George, David: 45, 48, 50, 54
London Gazette: 12, 14, 20, 21, 25, 37, 40, 44, 47, 61
Loseby, Captain: 38
Lutyens, Sir Edwin: 27

MacDonald, James Ramsay: 45, 48-50, 54, 55, 56, 66
Mansfield, Herbert: 24, 43
Marlborough House: 69, 70
Mary, Queen: 46
Mary, HRH the Princess Royal: 46, 69, 70
Masnieres: 38-40, 70
Melbourne Herald: 62
Military Cross: 25, 37, 59, 68
Minto, Cllr John: 56, 57, 62
Moline, Most Rev Robert W.: 72
Monckton, Sir Walter: 68
Morning Post, The: 60
Mosse, Lt-Col John: 21, 22
Mosse, Captain John W.E.: 21, 22, 24, 25

Neuve Chapelle: 10-12, 15, 18, 19, 28
Newcombe, L/Cpl Thomas: 20, 21
Niblett, Private Herbert: 70
Nicholas II, Tsar: 21
North, Ald Sir Jonathan: 13, 17, 18, 25, 41, 42, 59
Northstead, Manor of: 61

Oldfield, Private: 36

Pain, C Sgt B.: 18
Pascall, CSM Frederick W.: 36
Passchendaele: 38
Perth, Western Australia: 61-64, 71, 72
Pipes, Edward Barrand: 5
Poplar Board of Guardians: 17
Probyn, Gen Sir Dighton M.: 46
Punch: 58
Pulteney, Lt-Gen Sir William: 40

Queen Elizabeth the Queen Mother: 69, 70

Ratcliffe-on-the-Wreake, Leics: 49, 58
Rawlinson, Gen Sir Henry: 22
Returned Servicemen's League (RSL) of Australia: 72
Riley, Bishop A.L.: 72
Robinson, L/Cpl A.G.: 20, 21
Royal Air Force: 47
Royal Arsenal, Woolwich: 48, 49, 53
Royal Fusiliers Chronicle: 73
Royal Navy: 8, 47, 63
Russia: 34

Sarson, Col John Edward: 60
Shaw, Joseph C. and Family: 32
Shipley, Lt-Col C.A.L.: 71
Simpson, Cllr Herbert: 59
Smith, Mrs Abel: 18
Smith, Cpl Philip: 14
Smith, Walter: 14
Somme, Battle of: 22-24, 37
South Wigston, Leics: 22, 27
Stanley Chronicle: 32, 45
Swithland, Leics: 52, 53

Tank attacks: 22-24, 38
Tan-y-Castell, Caernarfon: 33
Tarry, Cpl W.: 10, 18, 19
Tees Garrison: 45, 46

Times, The: 46, 47, 48, 55, 59, 60, 72
Tower of London, HM: 70, 71

Unknown Warrior, The: 47

Victoria Cross: 10, 12, 13, 14, 15, 16, 17, 18, 27, 28, 40, 41, 42, 46, 47, 48, 51, 59, 60, 61, 62, 64, 65, 67, 68, 69, 70, 71

Wales, The Prince of (later Edward VIII): 27, 37, 41
Ward, George: 55, 57
War Memorials:
    Countesthorpe: 27, 51, 52
    Leicester: 25, 26
    Ratcliffe-on-the-Wreake, Leics: 49
    Swithland, Leics: 52, 53
    Thiepval: 26, 27
Welford Road Cemetery, Leicester: 6, 22, 31
West Australian: 72
Western Australia: 61-73
Westminster Abbey: 47, 48, 67
Willocks, Lt-Gen Sir James: 9
Williams, Aneurin: 45
Williams, Private John: 47
Windsor Castle: 70
Wood, Sir Kingsley: 50
Woolwich Garrison: 33
Woolwich Gazette & Plumstead News: 48, 50
Woolwich Town Hall: 48, 50
Worthington, Cllr Charles E.: 63
Wylly, Col Harold C.: 9

York, George Duke of (later George VI): 27, 46, 51, 52
Ypres: 37, 38

Zacks, Rabbi Rubin: 72